COUGAR

COUGAR

BY ROBERT GRAY

The Natural Life of a
North American Mountain Lion

A W. W. NORTON BOOK

GROSSET & DUNLAP

A NATIONAL GENERAL COMPANY

Publishers   *New York*

Dedicated to the memory of Frank Gray.
He taught his son a love of nature,
and he taught well.

Contents

Photographs

PART I

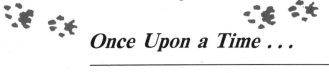

Once Upon a Time . . .

When I was ten years old, a cougar moved into our canyon, quietly and unannounced, like a ghost slipping among the trees. She came from the east, over by Lake Delmo country, and entered our canyon by crossing the divide. My father and I found her sign less than a mile from the cabin.

Our canyon was ideal cougar country, one of the wildest and most rugged canyons in western Montana. To me its walls were the steepest, its boulders the most massive and its stream by far the noisiest. At night I would fall asleep to the sound of that stream plunging among the rocks.

In those days the country for miles around us was wild—snow-covered mountain peaks; ice-cold

1

streams; forests of lodgepole pine and Douglas fir; secluded meadows; lakes rich with rainbow trout. There was wildlife—deer, elk, moose, bear, coyotes, even some wolves and many, many others. It was a world barely touched by man.

There was our place, of course—one small cabin and a placer mine. Half a mile downstream at the mouth of the canyon a dirt road twisted off toward civilization. Here and there you could find an abandoned prospector's cabin peacefully rotting back into the earth. Two miles south of us a railroad crossed the divide at Homestake, a settlement where the railroad's section gang and their families lived. There was a small ranch, Mr. Smith's place, near Homestake. Mr. Smith earned his living by bounty hunting and hiring out his team of horses.

And that was all. The rest of the country was as it always had been — a wilderness. Ideal for cougar.

My father and I learned about our cat one morning in July while we were out cutting wood. There was a clearing upstream from the cabin, a fifty-acre patch which had been burned over by a forest fire five years earlier. We went there to cut the dead trees into firewood.

That special morning began uneventfully enough. Bosco, our half-wolf, half-Airedale dog, ran on ahead, sniffing out rabbits and squirrels. A pair of eagles wheeled over us, making sure we stayed well away from their nest at the top of a nearby boulder. In a meadow at the head of the canyon, we came to a beaver dam. *SMACK!* One of the beavers heard us and slapped the water with his tail to warn the rest of his family. Bosco dashed to the pond, but all he found was a series of ripples showing where the beavers had dived to safety. Farther on, we saw several pines with their bark chewed away. They had been girdled by porcupines and would die.

At the edge of the burned clearing we stopped and looked. Usually, there were deer feeding in the clearing on the grass and new aspen trees which had grown back after the fire. That morning, a mule deer doe and her twin fawns bounded away. Bosco took after them, but he didn't have a chance in all that tangle of fallen timber.

My father and I set to work. He cut the smaller trees into four-foot lengths, and I dragged them to the edge of the clearing. Later, we would hire Mr. Smith's horses to haul the wood down to the cabin. Bosco disappeared among the downed trees to rummage for whatever good smells he could find. He generally worked quietly, but that morning he began to bark from the other side of the clearing. My father looked up from his saw.

"I wonder if he has a porcupine cornered over there," he said. "We better rescue him before he gets a nose full of quills."

We climbed over the fallen trees, scattered like giant jackstraws in the clearing. Bosco was standing beside a pile of brush and dirt. A deer's head stuck out from beneath it.

"Oh oh," my father said. "What have we here?"

He pushed the dog aside and raked away the debris. The deer was dead and partially eaten. Its intestines lay to one side and the rest of its entrails were missing. There were teeth marks on its throat. My father studied the carcass, then pushed back his hat and scratched his head. "It appears we have a new neighbor," he said.

"What is it?" I asked.

"A cougar. Look, all the sign is right—the buried carcass, the intestines and stomach cleaned out, the heart, lungs, liver, all eaten. And the teeth marks on the throat."

He removed his belt and looped it over Bosco's head. The dog had been nosing the ground back and forth near the deer, searching for the cat's trail.

"He might just find it," my father said. "And there's no sense in letting a perfectly good dog get himself killed."

Bosco tugged at the leash and my father followed him back into the clearing. Fifty feet away from the carcass, they stopped. My father called me.

"Here's where she pulled the deer down," he said, indicating the torn-up earth. "And there is where she dragged it out of the clearing." He pointed to the tufts of hair caught on logs, and to the bloodstains, already turning black. "I'd say she made the kill sometime yesterday afternoon."

He bent over a paw print in the earth. It was about five inches across—a large, flattened oval with three smaller ovals fanned out along one side.

"One of her front feet made that," my father said. "The pad of her foot made the large oval; the three smaller ones are her toes. There should be four toes. She's lost one."

We went back to the deer and covered it with dirt and brush. "No sense letting the flies get it after she worked so hard for her kill," my father explained.

"Will she come back?" I asked.

"As long as there's any meat and it doesn't spoil. And if we don't bother her."

"That means she's still around here." I glanced nervously into the forest.

My father laughed. "Maybe sitting on a ledge up there watching. But don't worry. The last thing she wants is to tangle with us, especially since we have Bosco with us. Now let's get back to work."

"But what are we going to do about her?" I asked.

My father tugged at the lobe of one ear as he always did when he was thinking serious thoughts. He motioned for me to sit beside him on a log. He spoke slowly as though to make sure I understood. "We're going to do nothing about her. Absolutely nothing. That cougar is our secret. We're not going to tell anybody—not your mother or sister. Nobody. You know why?" I shook my head. "Because if we did, the word would get back to Bill Smith. And he'd be up here in a flash with those hounds of his."

"You mean he'd kill her?"

"Just like that." My father snapped his fingers. "For the bounty. For the twenty-five dollars. Would you want that to happen?" I shook my head again. "Neither would I. I think our cougar has the same right to live as anybody else. She's part of nature. Maybe with her in the canyon we won't lose so many trees to porcupines, or have deer starving to death in winter. You just watch."

"You mean I'll get to see her?" I asked.

"Maybe, but I doubt it. There are people who have lived in cougar country all their lives, yet never seen one. Cougars are shy—ghost cats. But you'll know she's around if you keep your eyes open. You'll find sign—more kills like this one. You never know what you might find. But remember, no talking to anybody!"

So I kept quiet, but it wasn't easy, especially after school opened the following month. I ached to share the secret with the other kids. But then I remembered Mr. Smith and his hounds, and I kept my mouth shut.

I attended school at Homestake, in a tiny, one-room building that held all the grades—one through eight. Most of the pupils were from the railroad section gang families, and they didn't get into the mountains as much as I. The things I could have told them!

Depending on the time of year, I walked or skied the two miles from our cabin to school, and it was a rare day when I didn't find some new thing in the mountains around me. Then, after the cougar moved into our canyon, the daily trip promised even more adventure. I searched constantly for signs of her.

One day, I found her footprints in the snow beside the ones I had made on my way to school that very morning. I was being followed!

I told my father, and he said that cougars were very curious animals. They often followed people, especially children, according to the old stories. "Keep your eyes open," he advised. "There's a remote chance you'll see her."

But I didn't, at least not then. All I found were more tracks, sometimes twice a week or more, trailing behind me to within a half-mile of Homestake. There, without exception, they cut off through the forest toward the ridge which overlooked Mr. Smith's ranch.

I heard her, too. One evening late in December, my father and I were walking down to the mine. The night was clear and cold with a big, full moon in the sky. The snow squeaked under our feet. The coyotes which lived in the canyon were yipping back and forth as they did on most clear nights. A horned owl was hooting somewhere in the trees. Then, just as we passed under an overhanging rock, I heard the wildest, most unearthly sound imaginable. It sounded like a woman screaming in terror. A wild scream that rose higher and still higher, hanging there in the frozen air. On and on, echoing down the canyon and sending shivers up my back. Then it faded and was gone, leaving the night deathly still. No coyotes, no owl. I *knew* the cat was on the rock, ready to jump on us, and I started to run.

The Cougar (*Felis concolor*).
Wilford Miller

"Hey, come back here," my father called. "She's nowhere near. That came from way up on the west slope. Wasn't it beautiful? The most beautiful sound you've ever heard? Our friend is calling for a mate. Or maybe he's already showed up and she's greeting him. She's not the slightest bit interested in you right now."

But later that winter, she became interested in us and walked right up to our cabin.

By February, deep snow had forced the deer into the lower reaches of the canyons. They bunched up among the shelter of willows and under the pine trees and stayed alive by stripping away twigs and pawing through the snow to get at the old grass. The cougar followed them down from the high country, and she must have passed close to the cabin in her travels, close enough to smell the venison we had hanging in the root cellar. One night while I was doing my homework and Bosco was stretched out asleep in front of the fireplace, something jumped onto the roof. Something heavy. The boards creaked as whatever it was paced back and forth around the root cellar vent. Bosco jerked awake. He cocked his head and looked up at the roof. His hackles rose and he dashed to the door, barking. Whatever was on the roof bounded the length of the cabin and jumped off. My father took a lantern and went outside. He leaned a ladder against the cabin and climbed to the roof, where he called for me to come up. There, in the light from his lantern, I saw the cougar's prints in the snow. As my father had pointed out that day in the clearing, one of the toes on her left front foot was missing.

Then, one afternoon in late spring, I actually saw her. I was on my way home from school and, on impulse, cut back to the ridge overlooking Mr.

Smith's ranch. I wanted to learn what it was that made the cougar head that way whenever she followed me. But I didn't see anything special—just the ranch and beyond it, Homestake. I stretched out on a rock, and the combination of its warmth and the spring sun put me to sleep. An hour or so later I was wakened by the sun shining in my eyes. I blinked and turned my head to avoid the glare. At that moment, I saw her. She was lying on an outcropping about fifty feet away, sound asleep. She was a delicate tawny color with a pure white patch around her mouth. She had a heavy, black-tipped tail which lay stretched out behind her. She was sleek and smooth and looked like she owned the world.

I shifted to get a better look and my foot dislodged a rock, which clattered down the hill. The cougar snapped awake. She swung her head around and lay there for half a minute, gazing hard at me. Then she stood and jumped easily from the rock. In three graceful bounds she disappeared among the trees.

After that, I had to bite my tongue to keep from talking. But school finally closed and I rarely saw the other kids. I stayed back in the mountains most of the time, alone, exploring the cougar's country and looking for her sign. I found more kills—deer and porcupine mainly. I found a scrape in the saddle of the divide above our cabin—a pile of dirt with her droppings buried in it. One day I found a tree trunk scratched by her claws. All that summer I found evidence that she was still in the canyon, and, in fact, that she had restricted her movements.

"I suspect she has cubs now," my father said. "And they keep her close to home."

Oh, how desperately I wanted to see some of them!

In October I got my wish. One afternoon after school I saw a group of men gathered around Mr.

Smith's wagon, which was pulled up in front of the section house. I walked over and looked inside the wagon's box. Two cougar cubs lay there, side by side. Dead. Mr. Smith sat astraddle the wagon's seat, grinning down at his audience. He was a small man with a broken nose and tiny, pig-like eyes. Tobacco juice ran down the stubble on his chin.

"There's fifty dollars in bounty money layin' there," he bragged, pointing at the dead cubs. "Not bad for a mornin's work, even if it did cost me my best hound. When I seen his body torn open up there above the ranch, I knowed there was a cougar around."

Mr. Smith spat a line of tobacco juice down onto the spotted bodies lying in his wagon.

"Man, I sure do hate cougars," he said.

Well, it all happened many years ago. Now, civilization has found our little corner of Montana. Homestake is gone, torn down to the last board when the railroad company decided that it didn't need the section gang any longer. In the last few years a freeway has been cut through the mountains, close to the mouth of our canyon. Its traffic drowns out the sound of the stream that once lulled a ten-year-old boy to sleep at night. The trails he explored have been destroyed by jeeps and snowmobiles. His cabin is gone, burned by vandals. The canyon's boulders are defaced by splotches and splashes of paint. The beaver dam has disappeared, ripped apart by people who didn't care or didn't know better. And the roar of jet airliners comes and goes all day long.

It is unlikely that anybody ever again will hear a cougar screaming in the canyon. And it is the same all across our country; the cougars are almost gone, victims of "progress."

It wasn't always so. Just slightly more than four hundred years ago when white men first came to the

New World, there were cougars living in almost every part of the land, from southern Canada to the tip of South America, and from the Atlantic to the Pacific. They were equally at home in the highest mountains and at sea level, in tropical jungles and on snow-covered plains. Grassland and forest, swamp and desert, just about every place except the extreme northern Arctic was home to the cougars. They had the largest habitat of any American mammal.

Yet, because they lived only in the western hemisphere, cougars were unknown to Europeans until the fifteenth century. Christopher Columbus probably was the first white man to record their existence. During his fourth voyage, in 1502, while exploring the coast of Honduras and Nicaragua, he wrote that he saw "leones" (lions). Later, the white immigrants became all too familiar with them. In tiny settlements huddling along the Atlantic seaboard, cougars, along with Indians and wolves, became the symbol of the dreaded, unknown wilderness that lurked just beyond the cabin door. The cougars killed livestock and left the bodies to be found by the terrified settlers. They screamed out their unearthly songs from deep in the black, mysterious forest. They left large, round footprints in the snow and soft earth. Yet they were rarely seen, for they were the ghost cats. Understandably, they became the subjects of stories. Spun from half truths and outright lies, the stories always cast the cougar as villain. They hang on even today.

The logical conclusion of these stories is that cougars are vermin, less than worthless. They are to be killed on sight, exterminated. And, unfortunately, that is where the matter stands in much of the western hemisphere.

The truth is that cougars are simply a species of

wild animals. They are cats, members of that family of animals which includes all the cats from tabbies to tigers. Cougars are one of the six species called "great cats" because of their size. The other great cats are tigers, lions, leopards, cheetahs and jaguars.

The tiger is the largest of all cats. A fully grown Siberian tiger can weigh over eight hundred pounds and measure more than ten feet long, nose to tip of tail. We usually think of tigers as jungle animals, and one species, the Malayan tiger, does live in the tangled forests of southeastern Asia. But the Siberian's range is far to the north in Siberia and Manchuria. All tigers are very strong. In one instance, a Bengal tiger dragged away a buffalo which later required the combined strength of thirteen men to move.

The second largest cat is the African lion. A large individual might weigh five hundred pounds and measure ten feet long. At one time, lions lived throughout southern Europe, the Near East, in Asia, and, of course, Africa. Today, they are gone from all their former range except Africa and a tiny corner of India. The lion's title, "King of the Jungle," is as inaccurate as it is dramatic. The truth is that lions do not live in the jungle. Because they are hunting animals, they stay close to the game herds on the open plains.

Leopards have the largest range of all cats—most of Africa, eastward into southern Asia and north into Mongolia and Manchuria. Leopards vary in length from six to eight feet and weigh about one hundred fifty pounds depending on the race, of which there are several. One of the most beautiful is the Snow Leopard which lives in the Himalaya and Altai Mountains, more than 10,000 feet above sea level. It has soft, silvery hair marked with black rosettes. Snow Leopards are very rare and in danger of extinction, primarily because their coats are greatly prized by fashion designers.

Siberian tiger (*Panthera tigris longipilis*),
largest of the great cats.

The last of the Old World great cats is also the most unusual. It is the cheetah, an animal which seemingly barely fits in the cat family. The cheetah looks like a cross between a leopard and a greyhound dog. It has a small, round head, a slender body and long, thin legs. It is the smallest of the Old World great cats— eight feet long, and usually weighing less than one hundred pounds. Unlike other cats, the cheetah cannot retract its claws. Cheetahs are extremely fast runners, the fastest land animals on earth, and have been clocked at seventy miles an hour for short distances. They are easily tamed and, at one time, were considered the pets of royalty because so many were kept by kings and emperors as hunting animals. Today, wild cheetahs are found only on the plains and deserts of Africa and Iraq, and their numbers are decreasing. Like the Snow leopards and other spotted cats, cheetahs are prized for their coats.

Two of the world's great cats—jaguars and cougars —live only in the New World, the western hemisphere. Of the two, the jaguar is the larger, weighing about one hundred seventy-five to two hundred fifty pounds and measuring nine feet long. The smallest jaguars are found in the middle of the species' range —the tropics of Central and South America. Those living toward the extremes—north as far as the southwestern United States and south into Patagonia —tend to be a bit larger. Jaguars look very much like the leopards of the Old World but are stockier and have a larger head and shorter tail. Also, each of the rosettes along the jaguar's flanks has a black spot in the center.

Finally, there is the cougar, one of the smallest of the great cats. The cougar's length, tip of nose to tip of tail, is from seven to eight feet, and its weight is roughly one hundred and fifty pounds, although both

African lion (*Panthera leo*). Once
widespread throughout southern
Europe and Asia as well as Africa, the
lion now lives only in Africa and a
tiny corner of India.

Fred Schmidt/San Diego Zoo

Snow leopard (*Uncia uncia*). This beautiful cat lives above the tree line on rocky mountainsides in eastern Asia.

Jaguar (*Panthera onca*), largest of the American cats.

Fred Schmidt/San Diego Zoo

Cheetah (*Acinonyx jubatus*). Unlike other cats, the cheetah can run at high speed for almost half a mile pursuing its prey.

Fred Schmidt/San Diego Zoo

length and weight vary from one part of the species' enormous range to another. The largest cougar on record weighed two hundred and seventy-six pounds, and President Theodore Roosevelt killed one which weighed two hundred and twenty-seven pounds. A cougar killed in Montana in November 1970, equaled this size. As mentioned earlier, cougars lived from southern Canada to the tip of South America and from the Atlantic to the Pacific Oceans before the white men came to America. Today, they are still found along the north-south length of their range, but they have been virtually exterminated east of the Mississippi River in North America. There is a small population in Florida's Everglades—one hundred to three hundred animals—a few in other southern states, the Great Lakes area, the Northeast, and a small number—perhaps ten to twenty—in New Brunswick and eastern Canada. But except for these isolated groups, North America's cougars have been pushed back into remote islands of wilderness in the west. We don't know how many lived in the Americas when the white men first landed; the number must have been well in the hundreds of thousands, maybe even a million or more. And because cougars are truly ghost cats, living far from man in the wilderness, we don't know how many are left today. Authorities place the number between 7,500 and 18,000 in the United States and Canada. There is no accurate guess as to the population in Central and South America. But it is safe to say that the total number of cougars in the western hemisphere is decreasing.

As a cat, the cougar belongs to a group of animals which traces its ancestry back about forty million years, to the time when a creature named *Dinictis* appeared on earth. Whereas the distinctive pattern

American Museum of Natural History. Painting by Charles R. Knight

Dinictis, the prehistoric cat, chasing a
Protoceras, an extinct ancestor of today's
chevrotain, a tiny, deer-like animal.

Smilodon, an extinct sabretoothed tiger of
South America.

American Museum of Natural History. Painting by Charles R. Knight

of other carnivores (meat-eating animals) had yet to develop, *Dinictis* looked very much like a modern cat. He was about the size of today's lynx and had long, sharp canine teeth (eyeteeth) and retractile claws. *Dinictis,* in turn, had evolved from a still earlier group of carnivores called the *Miacids,* and a very fortunate line of evolution it was, for the resulting combination of claws and teeth proved to be extremely efficient hunting tools. And in the millions of years that followed, as other animals underwent tremendous evolutionary changes, the cat family remained more or less unchanged.

It consisted of two main lines of evolution. One led to the development of extremely long upper canine teeth. The most dramatic result of this line was the prehistoric sabretoothed tiger, also called the stabbing cat. There were several species of this creature, and the best known was an animal about the size of a lion, with powerful forequarters and weak hindquarters. Its upper canines were more than six inches long and extended below the chin when the mouth was closed. The sabretooths became extinct just a few thousand years ago, possibly because they were slow-moving animals which would have been a disadvantage in hunting.

The second, and successful evolutionary line of development from *Dinictis* led to cats with small canine teeth and bodies designed for speed. The first of these "typical" cats appeared about ten million years ago.

Today's cats are roughly divided into two groups. One, called *Leo,* has eyes with round pupils, and a throat structure which allows for roaring but no purring. Lions, tigers, leopards and jaguars belong to the *Leo* group. The second group, *Felis,* consists of cats which do not roar but are capable of purring. For the most part, this group has eyes with vertical pupils. There are many species in the *Felis* group, among them the cougar. The closest living relatives of all cats are the civets and hyenas.

Very early in the development of the carnivores, back there some fifty million years beginning with the *Miacids,* Nature made certain, basic decisions regarding their evolutionary paths. These decisions set the life style of the different groups. One group of carnivores, for instance, returned to the sea from which all life had emerged hundreds of millions of years earlier. These marine carnivores became the whales, seals and walruses we have today. In forsaking the land, they gradually lost their legs, a fact which settled forever the definition of home for them. While it is true that seals and walruses can haul out onto dry land and even flounder around a bit, their natural element is water. And for a whale of any size from the enormous blue whale to the smallest dolphin, to leave the sea is out of the question. He doesn't have even the most elementary equipment to make this possible.

In much the same way as marine carnivores became locked into their life style, so the terrestrial carnivores traveled along evolutionary paths which established the manner in which they would live. Dogs and cats provide an excellent comparison.

Dogs—the wolves, coyotes, foxes, jackals, and so forth—developed long, slender legs and jaws which were adapted for snapping and slashing.

The cats developed as animals with short, strong legs; extremely powerful claws which can be retracted; and short jaws.

Dogs became cursorial, meaning they became runners capable of racing along for mile after mile, literally running their prey to death. Cats developed into sprinters, able to dash at tremendous speeds but for only a short time.

The dogs nip and tear at the flanks and legs of their prey as they run behind them; cats leap and hold on with jaws and claws.

These two hunting styles dictate the social life of dogs and cats. Many wild dogs—wolves, for instance —live in packs and hunt cooperatively. Several animals join together to run down the prey. The hunting unit is not an individual animal; it is the pack. In cursorial hunting, several animals can do what one animal cannot.

Cats, on the other hand, hunt best alone—sneaking up, crouching, dashing and pouncing, then breaking the victim's neck, strangling or smothering it. So, with the exception of African lions, which live in groups called prides, the cats are loners, living out solitary lives. And even in the lion prides the hunting is done by one or two lionesses at a time, not the entire group.

Because dogs hunt and live in packs, their social life is much different than that of cats. Pack members are friendly and cooperative. Everyone helps to raise and train the babies. There is a pack leader whose authority is absolute.

The cats know of no such social structure, again except for African lions. Individuals of the other species come together only to mate, then the female is left to bear and raise her cubs by herself. She does not welcome other members of her species into her territory, neither does she cooperate with them. It is every cat for itself.

Cougars are typical cats, both physically and in their life style. If anything, they are even more solitary and secretive than the other species. Except for rare, accidental sightings, the only time a person is apt to see a wild, live cougar is when it has been treed by dogs or is caught in a trap.

Yet the cougar is the most beautiful of all great cats. At least I think so, but maybe my judgment was prejudiced on that warm, spring day many years ago when I awoke to see our cougar sprawled sunning on a rock.

The first impression one has in seeing a cougar is of a fawn-colored, low-slung animal with short, heavy legs and an extremely long tail. The legs are very powerful with heavy layers of muscle rippling just beneath the skin. The feet are enormous—broad pads that carry the cat silently among the duff on the forest floor. The tail is truly very long—the longest, heaviest tail of all cats—up to one-third of the cougar's total length. A patch of black hair grows at its tip. The cougar's head seems too small for the rest of her. It is round, with a pair of dark brown, rounded ears. The muzzle is flanked by a mass of dark hair which outlines what is called the "butterfly" pattern —a patch of white hair which seems to wing from each side of the cat's upper lip and chin. The tip of her black nose is a delicate pink color. Finally, there are the cougar's eyes, which many people consider to be the most beautiful of any in the animal world. They are large and almond-shaped with large, dark pupils and of a color which defies description. It is a translucent, living, greenish-gold, or as the naturalist/writer, Ferris Weddle, described it, a "gooseberry green." These eyes seem to miss nothing. They can be alert and intense, as when the cougar is tracking and sneaking up on her prey. They might be equally alert but with a businesslike steadiness, as when she is dashing toward her prey. The eyes appear almost humorous when the cat is investigating something new; and they are gentle and soft when she is relaxed, perhaps sprawled in the sun. But whatever their mood the eyes are always alive, the most alive - appearing part of this most beautiful animal.

The cougar has at least forty names, far more than any other American mammal. The most popular include cougar, puma, mountain lion, panther, painter, catamount, Mexican tiger and deer tiger. Among the Indians the cat seems to have had names which, when translated into English, indicate how these early Americans saw the animal. "Greatest of Wild Hunters." "Lord of the Forest." "The Cat of God." "Father of Game." In Central and South America the cougar is called simply "leon."

Fortunately, within all this confusion, there is one name which is accepted every place in the world, *Felis concolor,* the cougar's scientific name. It is based on the science of taxonomy, a system of classification invented almost two hundred years ago by the Swedish scientist, Linnaeus. In taxonomy, living beings—plants and animals—are classified according to their likenesses or differences and become more precisely defined until one, and only one, group of plants or animals is being described. For instance, the cougar, first of all is neither a plant nor a mineral, so falls within the third basic classification, an animal. It is a member of the animal kingdom. Next, because it has a spinal cord, it is classified as a chordate. Because it is warm-blooded, has hair, bears its young alive, then nurses them, it is a mammal. It eats meat, so is a carnivore. As a cat, it is a member of the *Felidae* family. It is in the genus, *Felis,* and finally, its species name is *concolor. Felis concolor,* the great cat which is the subject of this book and which we shall call "cougar."

But all of this—the cat's name, the color of its coat and eyes, its length and weight—tell us very little about the cougar. It is as though your family and friends had only the same facts about you—name, color, size. Hardly enough to know you as a person.

So it is with the cougar. We must go beyond a mere

physical description to learn what kind of animal it is. How does it live? What does it eat and how does it get its food? Who are its enemies? How does it protect itself? How does it care for its babies? How does its homeland influence its life? If we can answer these kinds of questions, then we will begin to know the cougar.

What we are interested in is behavior, the subject of a new science called ethology. For all but the last few years, man has studied animal behavior in artificial situations, primarily in zoos and laboratories. But, in most instances, the behavior he saw in these captives was not at all like that which he glimpsed in animals living in the wild. So finally, someone suggested that perhaps the very fact of being in captivity influences the animals. For instance, baboons have been studied for a long time, but always in zoos. From what scientists saw there, they decided that baboons are aggressive, vicious animals, obsessed with sex. Yet, when the same species are studied as they go about their lives in the wild, they are seen to be cooperative, friendly, very loving of their babies, well organized into troops and no more interested in sex than any other species.

So in the last few years, ethologists have taken their studies into the field, right into the animals' homes. From these expeditions we are learning much that we didn't know about grizzlies, wolves, chimpanzees, gorillas, lions and many other animals. Only recently has field work been started on cougars, and there still is much to be done, for they are difficult subjects. The most detailed work as of 1970 has been done by Dr. Maurice Hornocker and his associates at the University of Idaho. A picture is forming and the story it tells is of an animal far different from the bloodthirsty demon of myth and folk tale.

In the following section I shall try to tell this story.

The people and some of the situations in it are real; the rest of the story is drawn from the storyteller's imagination and the hours he spent studying reports and talking with experts.

So if all of it didn't happen, it could have.

PART II   *Felis*

When I was ten years old, a cougar moved into our canyon, quietly and unannounced, like a ghost slipping among the trees.

The Search

A breeze, pungent with the perfume of pines, flowed out onto the alpine meadow. It jostled the summer grasses and wild flowers as it passed, disturbing a work force of diligent bees probing for nectar. It bowed the heavy grasses, already heading out in the hot July sunshine, then climbed the hillside at the meadow's southern flank where it slipped between the pine trees standing there like a regiment of green-clad soldiers. At the top of the hill it whirled among a jumble of boulders cluttered like giant tenpins along the crest. Then it passed down the other side, and for a brief moment, cooled the faces of the two men who were struggling up the hill.

Each of the men carried a rifle, and the smaller also held the leash of a hound dog who nosed each squir-

rel hole in the warm hillside. The small man had a broken nose and tiny, pig-like eyes. Tobacco juice trickled down the gray stubble growing on his chin. He was a mountain man, a bounty hunter. His companion was large and paunchy, soft from too many years spent at a desk. He was a businessman from the East who had hired the hunter to guide him to a cougar. "I want a pelt for the wall of my den," he had boomed. Now, on the hot hillside, he stopped and mopped his brow. "Whew! I wish that breeze had kept up. It surely felt good."

The hunter looked at him, disgusted. "Mr. Williams, I warned you to keep quiet once we got on this here hill. With just one hound dog we're gonna have enough trouble gettin' your cougar. You keep on makin' all this noise and you'll drive away every critter on the mountain."

The businessman became incensed. He was not used to having people tell him what to do; after all, he was a very important person back East. "Well, Mr. Smith, it wasn't my idea to come out with only one dog," he said. "You're supposed to be the professional hunter. Why didn't we bring more hounds?"

The bounty hunter squirted a line of tobacco juice onto the hillside. "Like I said, my good bitch is whelpin' and I'm not about to run the danger of losin' those pups of hers. I told you we should have waited a few days until I could borrow some dogs."

"I have other things to do," Mr. Williams puffed. "It was now or never. Anyway, you were eager enough to snap up that hundred dollars I offered."

The bounty hunter snorted and led the way toward the crest of the hill. At the top, he stood motionless, studying the meadow below. Suddenly he dragged the hound to him and motioned for his client to move nearer. He put a finger to his lips for silence, then pointed.

A mature, adult cougar—huge paws, round head, widespread ears, alert eyes and the distinctive butterfly pattern spanning the muzzle.   *San Diego Zoo*

Below them on the meadow, a cougar was crouched in the grass, feeding on a porcupine.

"We're in luck," the hunter whispered. He unleashed the hound and slapped his rump. "Go git her!" he commanded.

The dog had neither seen nor smelled the cat, but upon being slapped, he snapped alert. When he saw the cougar on the meadow below, he raced down toward her, yelping. The two men galloped along behind.

The cougar looked up from her meal, saw the hound, and spun for the safety of the forest. The hound lunged at her flanks, missed and tumbled into the grass.

On the hillside, Mr. Williams suddenly stopped running. He sank to one knee and whipped the rifle to his shoulder.

"No! No!" the bounty hunter screamed. "Let the dog tree her first."

But the businessman was inexperienced in cougar hunting. He fired.

His bullet grazed the cat's shoulder, bowling her over. It went on and struck the dog, who was struggling to his feet for another lunge at the cat. The dog flipped over in the air and fell dead; the cougar sprang upright and ran into the forest.

The sound of the shot echoed like a thunderclap from the hills encircling the meadow. It frightened a mallard duck which had been feeding in the stream. The duck exploded into the air and streaked away. A group of bleary-eyed frogs had been dozing in the sun. *PLOP! PLOP!* They dived into the water. A noisy jay fell silent among the trees on the far side of the meadow. The echoes of the shot faded, leaving just the sounds of the two men trudging onto the scene.

The bounty hunter stepped up to his dead dog. He

turned the body over with the toe of one boot. He glared at the businessman. "Big hunter from the East!" he snarled.

"I saw the cat running and thought she would get away," Mr. Williams explained.

"Well, she sure did, and all we've got to show is one dead dog."

"Oh, don't worry. I'll pay for your dog. Now, let's get after the cougar."

The hunter snorted. "Mister, you might as well forget it. That cat is in the next county by now."

But he was wrong. Felis the cougar was crouched on a rock high above them, watching their every move.

The hunters had taken her completely by surprise, a most unusual and dangerous thing to happen to a cougar. But Felis had been upwind, so didn't hear or smell them as they came over the hill. And she was busy at the porcupine, her first meal in several days. Also, she was a young animal, inexperienced in the ways of her enemy, man. But because she was a creature of the wilderness where the law was to stay alert or die, there were no acceptable excuses for carelessness. The only reason she escaped was because the businessman had made a mistake. If he had not killed the dog, probably she would have been tracked down.

Despite her carelessness, when she did act, her movements were immediate and right. At the first warning of danger every nerve and muscle in Felis' body reacted. After the bullet knocked her down, she was on her feet at once, bounding in ten- and fifteen-foot leaps for the safety of the forest.

She dashed up the hillside, zigzagging among the trees, leaping fallen logs, and crashing through the bushes in her frenzy to escape. High on the hillside she burst out of the forest and onto the talus below the summit. She clambered up the loose slope and at the top, stopped for a moment to look back. Nothing seemed to be chasing her. She was breathing hard from her run, but, spurred on by fear, she ran along the crest toward the boulders that lay piled like ten-pins. She slipped in between them and slithered along the passageways formed by the jumbled rocks. She reached a dead end, stopped, and seemed about to retrace her path. Then she turned and leaped more than fifteen feet up onto the face of the boulder. Her claws dug for a purchase on the rough granite. She fought her way to the top, and without stopping, dropped to the ground on the other side. At the far end of the rock pile she came to one boulder, larger than the others, which hung out over the meadow far below. Its face was sheer, a fifty-foot cliff of granite with specks of mica glistening like gold in the sunshine. A ledge ran across the face of the boulder. Felis jumped onto it and worked her way to the platform where the ledge widened out. Beyond the platform, the boulder's face was smooth, polished by a thousand years of snow and rain. This was trail's end for the cougar. She turned and backed against the boulder, as far under the overhang as possible. She crouched and waited. If danger were following, it had to come across the ledge she had taken. She was as ready for it as she could be.

She was exhausted. Her escape had been very strenuous, a run of almost half a mile, and most of it uphill. Her chest heaved and her mouth hung open as she panted.

The bullet wound was beginning to bother her. It was minor, a mere crease across the shoulders that would heal in a few days, but in the meantime it burned like fire.

Yet neither her exhaustion nor the wound was important now. There was danger nearby, a threat that was related somehow to the two-legged creatures and their dog. And there was the horrifying noise like thunder which had flung her into the grass. She must stay alert.

From her perch on the boulder Felis could see the meadow, far below, and the two tiny specks which were the men who had brought trouble to her. She watched them as they stood arguing and waving their arms. Then the smaller one turned and walked back across the meadow. The larger man followed him. They entered the forest and climbed the hill. Felis saw them once more as they crossed the brow of the hill; then they disappeared down the other side.

The meadow lay quiet. The mallard duck which had been frightened by the rifle fire, winged past the rock on which Felis crouched. It circled the meadow and plopped into the stream. The frogs hopped back onto the bank to continue their sunbathing.

Slowly, Felis relaxed. She stretched her forelegs in front of her body. Her tail quit twitching and she draped it around her. She tried to lick the wound on her shoulder but couldn't reach it. She lowered her head onto her outstretched legs. The boulder's heat seeped through the thick, white fur on her belly, lulling her and quieting the danger signals which had sent her fleeing up the mountainside. She closed her eyes and fell asleep.

Did she dream? We don't know. Do animals dream? Watch a dog as it lies sleeping, yipping softly and moving its legs. Is it dreaming of chasing a rabbit? Or notice a house cat as it suddenly jerks in its sleep. Pouncing on a mouse?

Maybe Felis did dream as she lay sleeping on the sun-warmed boulder.

It could be that she dreamed of her mother, brother and sister. Certainly, aside from the recent

San Diego Zoo

This nine-month-old, zoo-bred cougar kitten
still has spots on its front legs, but they are
disappearing.

horror of her experience on the meadow, they were the most immediate realities in her short life. Yet they were gone, probably never to be seen again. For at two years of age, Felis, barely an adult, was leaving her family.

It was a natural separation, one which each cougar must face. But that did not make it any easier for the young cat whose entire life had been filled by her mother and litter mates. When she was hungry, mother was there to supply milk and, later, meat. When she was ready to play, there were the other cubs, eager for a romp. And on the occasion when she had her first great adventure, the family was there to love and comfort her. It had happened when she was one year old and spending part of her time exploring. One day she moved along the trail which climbed the saddle in the mountains bordering her mother's territory. At the top of the divide, there was a trap, put there by the bounty hunter. It was carefully concealed just below ground, with twigs arranged on each side of it so that a cougar would almost surely step in it, especially if the animal had had no previous experience with a trap. Felis had none and she got caught. But only by the outermost toe of her left forepaw. In her panic, when she reared back to escape from the trap, her toe was torn away. She had run back to mother, who washed the wounded foot with her tongue.

Love, food, warmth. These were her family.

Then, during the summer of her second year, she saw her mother change. The adult female was coming into heat again, the first time since she had conceived the litter of which Felis was a member. For almost two years she had concentrated on caring for the three cubs. Now she wanted to mate again, have a new family. But first, she had to be rid of the old one. She became irritable and short tempered. In-

Mule deer (*Odocaileus virginianus*), the favorite food of cougars.

Moose (*Alces alces*), largest member of the deer family and another of the cougar's prey.

stead of sharing meat with her cubs, she drove them away from a kill. When they wanted to play, she cuffed them, hard. One morning she turned on Felis and trounced her, snarling, biting and swatting the bewildered cat.

So Felis left. Instinctively, she realized that she had to make a home of her own, far removed from her mother's territory. She moved south, through the saddle in the mountains where she had lost a toe in the bounty hunter's trap. The first night away from her old home she was high in the mountains, alone and hungry. Although she was on her own, she had yet to perfect the craft of hunting. In her two years, she had never killed a deer or elk or moose. Her hunting had been confined to small animals—mice, ground squirrels and rabbits. Yet in the end, deer would be the basis of her diet.

On the sixth day away from her family, she arrived at the alpine meadow where she found and killed the porcupine as she had seen her mother kill them, with a quick flip of the paw. It was there that the hunters found her crouched over her first meal in a week.

So, because so much of her short life was associated with her family, Felis could well have been dreaming of them as she slept on the sun-warmed boulder overlooking the meadow. But this is only guesswork. Maybe she didn't dream at all. Maybe her sleep that afternoon was a black void in which her strong young body recharged its muscles and nerves after the experience on the meadow. We don't know.

Late in the afternoon, a red-tailed hawk flew up to the platform where Felis was sleeping. The hawk had a nest across the meadow and each day left the four eggs she was incubating to come to the platform to search for mice in the meadow below. Any mouse brave or stupid enough to leave the safety of its runway was sure to be caught. With her keen vision—

eighty times more powerful than a man's—she saw
the slightest movement and would swoop down.
Now as she braked for a landing on her hunting platform, she suddenly realized it was occupied. She
wheeled away. *KREE! KREE!* Her scream of annoy-
ance awoke Felis the cougar. The hawk winged past
again, and the sunlight gleamed from her four-foot-
long wings and the rufus-colored tail for which she
was named. *KREE!*

Felis instinctively recognized that the bird posed
no threat to her safety. Neither, because it was safely
aloft, did it represent a meal. So she was merely
mildly curious as the hawk continued to fly by,
screaming her anger. So far as Felis was concerned,
the most important fact was that her own belly was
empty. Her earlier fear, raised by the hunters and
their dog, lay far back on the other side of sleep, in
another world, another life. Like all wild animals, she
lived in the present, moment by moment, and at this
moment she was hungry.

She would never forget the experience with the
hunters, just as she would always remember the trap
into which she had once blundered. It was all part of
the wisdom she must acquire if she were to live. But,
for now, the danger had passed.

She stood and stretched, arching her back as a
house cat does when it first awakens. The wound
across her shoulders was stiff and sore. She yawned
and sat on her haunches, watching the angry hawk as
it wheeled in front of her. Then she picked her way
back across the ledge, jumped to the ground and
moved into the forest. The hawk settled onto the
platform, ruffled her feathers and sat unblinking, surveying her domain.

Felis emerged from the trees and padded across
the meadow toward the porcupine she had killed. It
lay as she had left it, on its back with the unprotected

belly torn open by her claws. She crouched beside it
and ate everything but the stomach, intestines and,
of course, the skin with its coat of quills. But the
porcupine had been young and small, hardly a full
meal for the cougar. At two years of age Felis
weighed eighty pounds, about one-half of what she
would weigh when fully grown, and she needed
large amounts of food. She walked over to the dead
dog and sniffed it. It was covered with the smell of
the hunters. In fact, the entire area around the dog
was filled with the strange odor. Felis sniffed the
grass where the two men had stood arguing. Somewhere inside of her the scent registered, forever
after to be associated with the fear she had experienced. She laid her ears back and snarled.

Later in the afternoon she caught a hare, com-
monly called a snowshoe rabbit, among the willows
at the lower end of the meadow. After eating, she sat
on her haunches and washed her face, licking one
paw, then wiping it back and forth across the but-
terfly-patterned muzzle. Back and forth, leaning her
tawny head into her paw, looking like a soft, over-
sized kitten.

Her grooming done, Felis walked to the stream
and drank, leaning forward to lap up the water with
her huge, sandpaper-rough tongue. Then she leaped
lightly across the stream and followed it along the
narrow canyon it had carved through the mountains
over the past ten thousand years. When the moon
rose later that night, Felis was still traveling, picking
her way among the rocks which littered the canyon's
bottom. She was looking for a home.

Few of nature's creatures, from field mouse to
man, are free of the need for a place of their own, a
territory. To the field mouse, territory is a tiny burrow and an elaborate system of runways through the
grass. For man, it is a house, a community and a

nation. A male elephant seal has as his territory a few square yards on a rocky beach. For certain fish it is the area surrounding the pebbles they have piled on the bottom of a stream or pond. Territoriality—the drive to find a place—is almost as old as animal life itself!

And since it is so old, there must be a good reason for its existence. Drives and habits which do not contribute to the welfare of a species don't last long in the evolutionary relay race. And that is what survival is—a relay race in which one generation passes along genes to the next generation. It is literally a race of life or death. If the genes are the best the species has and if they adapt the new generation to the ever-changing conditions of its environment, enough babies probably will survive to breed children of their own. But if the genes do not meet the needs of the times the species eventually will disappear. Actually, in the two billion years of life on earth, far more species have slipped into extinction than have survived. Evolution demands the absolute best from its relay runners and it is totally unforgiving.

So the territorial drive has a very important part to play in survival. First, it assures that the best males will become fathers. It works this way: Those males who can establish and hold territory are the strongest, the wisest, the bravest ones of the species—whatever is required to find and hold a piece of property. The females gravitate or are driven to the males with territory. These males mate. The ones without territory get no wives. So the best males father the babies; thus those genes which are most important for species' survival are passed on.

Territoriality is so strong a drive that it actually overshadows the sexual urge in many species. Among birds called lapwings, for instance, the males squabble constantly as they establish and defend territories during breeding season. But when these same males gather at a feeding station, even when there are females present, they do not fight, but feed peacefully side by side. Then, as soon as they fly back into their territories, they start fighting again, not over female lapwings, who might still be at the feeding trough, but over their individual territories.

The territorial drive also helps species' survival by assuring there will be enough room to bear and raise families. Since the family chores include finding food, a well-spaced population of animals guarantees that the range will not be overeaten.

Despite the amount of conflict which territoriality seems to cause in a species, it actually reduces the amount of actual fighting which goes on. Animals recognize and respect each other's territory, and their courage fades as they move farther into a territory which is not their own. The owner's role is to drive the intruder away, not to kill him. Once territories are established and their defenses tested and proved sound, the species can get about its main business, breeding the next generation of animals. Certainly, this has survival value, for if competition for a mate were a constant battle to the death, the males would gradually be killed off, very little breeding would take place, and the species would suffer and perhaps disappear.

Yet there are a few species which conduct all-out fights, as though the drive to defend territory had become distorted and were an end in itself. The Siamese fighting fish offer an example of this, often fighting to the death. On the other hand, certain animals, such as the howler monkeys, conduct highly ritualized, noisy "wars." These involve tremendous racket and running about, but no one is hurt and no physical contact made. Still the "wars" accomplish their purpose—territorial defense. Man's wars, tragically, although equally as ritualized as the monkeys', are bloody, inhumane affairs in which thousands, even millions of people are killed or maimed. In looking at this horrid aspect of human behavior can we honestly say that man is not subject to the same blind, instinctive urges which drive the tiny Siamese fighting fish and the howler monkey?

Scientists have only recently begun to study territoriality, and what they have found sheds some interesting light on animal behavior.

Bird songs, for instance. For thousands of years, we humans have thrilled to the sound of birds singing in the wilderness. We have called it beautiful, which, of course, it is, since beauty is whatever we claim it to be. But at this point we get into trouble. Just because we consider bird songs beautiful, we assume that the birds do also. We think that their singing expresses the birds' joy and love of life. Far from it. Most bird songs are warnings. The red-winged blackbird swaying on his reed in the marsh and a robin perched high in the maple tree are saying the same thing: "This is my territory. Stay out!" In other words, the singing is one way of defending territory by telling other blackbirds and robins that it is occupied.

However, we must not think that, just because bird songs do not fit into our romantic notions about them, they are any the less beautiful. Beauty, as a poet once said, is in the eye of the beholder. And the outstanding naturalist, Konrad Lorenz, wrote, "The rainbow is no less beautiful because we have learned to understand the laws of light refraction to which it owes its existence. ..."

The actual defense of territory is an interesting aspect of animal behavior. For instance, scientists have learned that the strength of this drive depends on what part of the territory is involved. There is a fish—the stickleback—which selects a territory and builds a nest of aquatic plants. He lures several females into the nest to lay eggs which he fertilizes. Then, during the time that the eggs are incubating he drives away any stickleback——male or female—who enters the territory. But the vigor of his defense is related to the distance the intruder is from the nest, which is in the exact center of the stickleback's territory. The invader will always retreat from the defender, but as he is pushed back closer to the territorial boundary he becomes braver and more difficult to push around. If the battle should cross over into his territory, the tables are turned and the former invader suddenly becomes the defender, who drives away the stickleback who was pursuing him mere moments earlier.

How do the sticklebacks know where their boundaries are? We can't say, but the fish recognize them, just as humans know where the territorial boundaries are for them—the doors of a person's house, and his property lines. The old adage, "A man's house is his castle," is one way of saying that a person has the right to defend his home, his territory.

Cities and states are divided by well-defined boundaries. And, of course, national borders do the same thing. But even these seemingly exact boundaries leave much to be desired. What happens, for instance, when a nation borders on the ocean? How far does its territory extend out to sea? Traditionally, it has been three miles, a figure arrived at several hundred years ago when the biggest cannons could fire no farther than that. But today, with missiles and bombers, the three-mile limit has no meaning. Many nations now claim that their territory extends up to two hundred miles seaward, or to put it another way, to the outer limits of the continental shelf. There is another question. How far into the air does a nation's territory extend? Before the airplane was invented, this question was pointless. But now, with high flying jets, rockets and satellites, it is a question which becomes increasingly important. For the present, it seems that the rule of thumb is, "If you are able to shoot down whatever is flying over you, that object is in your territory." But this is a poor rule which could cause serious trouble some day.

Aside from man, animals seem to have no such problems in defining territory. If an individual of a given species is on another individual's territory, he realizes it and knows that he must be ready to fight or flee if the legitimate owner shows up.

In some cases animal territorial borders are so obvious that even we humans can recognize them. Wolf packs, for instance, mark trees, bushes and rocks with scent from glands near the base of their tails. So do other canines. Territorial primates have recognizable, if less distinctly marked, physical borders—this tree, that rock—and both the owners and neighboring primates of the same species know where the borders are. A herd of antelope in Africa, migrating with the maturing of the grass, maintains and defends a territory which moves along—large enough to feed the herd, small enough to defend— a territory that is defined by the outer limits of the herd itself. The red-winged blackbird has a territory which is bordered by a certain stick, a tree, a pole sticking out of the water, and so long as he can defend it against other blackbirds, it is his.

Since the whole point of territoriality is survival, and since it is so deeply ingrained, it is not surprising that we find territorial behavior developing early in the young. Wolf pups learn to recognize and make scent marks long before they are sexually mature. The wolf pup grows up in a situation where the territory belongs to the entire pack, not to any individual within it. The pup must establish a place for himself

Robert Gray

As the cougar explores her territory, she truly
seems a ghost cat, working quietly through
the forest.

in the pack, but he is not faced with the problem of finding a territory. The pack did that long before he was born. As an adult, his job will be to help defend it.

But for species which live solitary lives, the situation is quite different. Each individual animal must set up a territory of its own. Usually, this means leaving home and finding a place which is empty or occupied by an old, weak animal who can be defeated. In this type of social structure those animals which manage to establish and defend territories can be considered successful. Those which do not, live pathetic lives as failures—drifters who are driven from place to place by the owners of the territories they invade. If the drifter is a female she is truly a failure, for the odds are that she will never fill her role in the species; she will never mate and have a family.

So Felis the cougar was urged along by one of the most basic of all drives as she padded down the narrow canyon that moonlit night. Her quest was nothing less than to find and establish a place for herself in her wilderness world.

At dawn, she reached the canyon's mouth. A small, man-made lake lay there, locked into the mountains by a dam. The lake was used to irrigate farms and ranches in a large valley several miles to the east. And it was popular with fishermen who hiked up from the valley to catch the rainbow trout it contained.

But on that morning when Felis moved warily out of the canyon the lake was quiet—smooth and polished in the flat light which precedes the sun. A faint mist rose from its surface. Ducks chattered softly to themselves as they paddled among the rushes growing in the shallows. A fish jumped, sending concentric circles of ripples fanning out across the water. *PLOP!* The fish caught an insect and fell back below

the surface. A mule deer buck stood at the water's
edge, nibbling the tender tip ends of willows. Its
summer coat was a rich, reddish brown, a condition
which hunters refer to as being "in the red," and its
antlers still were velveted. The buck had shed its
previous year's antlers after the rutting season. In
April the new set had started to grow. Now, in mid-
summer, they were covered by an envelope of vel-
vet-soft skin which nourished them and which would
later be discarded. The deer looked up from its feeding, saw Felis and dashed away with the stiff-legged,
bouncing gait characteristic of mule deer.

But he was in no danger. The young cougar was
absolutely no match for him. Her first deer kills
would be of very old or very young animals and many
months would pass before she had enough hunting
experience to threaten a fully grown buck.

After the deer disappeared Felis walked down to
the lake to drink. The ducks swam out to the safety
of open water. A muskrat broke cover and waddled
to his burrow. Two cottontail rabbits dashed from the
willows. A second mule deer bounced away from the
edge of the lake, and there were tracks of still others
who had come to feed and drink.

With such an ample supply of prey animals, the
lake and its surrounding mountains was an ideal
place for a cougar to make its home, so ideal in fact,
that two cats had already staked out their territories,
one on the north side of the lake, the other on the
south. Felis was in the north cougar's territory, and
before the morning was over, she made contact with
the owner. The resident cougar was an old female,
traveling with her one-year-old cubs. Normally,
female cougars do not seem to mind if their territory
overlaps that of another female. The ladies get along
by simply ignoring each other. But the cat which
Felis contacted was fifteen years old. Her teeth were

worn back and she had difficulty hunting for herself
and the two cubs which trailed along behind her.
The three cats were thin and wasted and very irritable. When Felis ran into them high on the mountain
beside the lake, they were tearing apart a rabbit
which the mother had managed to capture. When
the old female saw Felis ambling through the forest
she swung around and snarled at her. Felis took off,
bounding down the hill, across the stream and up the
other side, well out of the territory which had
seemed so promising but which contained such ill-
tempered neighbors.

Early afternoon found her traveling westward
over the mountains, following a series of game trails.
The country she was entering was much rougher
than the relatively gentle hills around the lake. Felis
was working her way up to the Continental Divide,
the backbone of rocks and mountain peaks which
separates the drainage systems of the continent. The
land she traveled through lay to the east of the Divide. Its hundreds of tiny streams eventually became
three rivers which joined near a town named Three
Forks located at the head of the Missouri River. The
Missouri emptied into the Mississippi, which flowed
into the Gulf of Mexico, two thousand miles and
more from the Divide. On the west side of the Divide
there was a broad, mile-high valley named Silver
Bow for the stream which looped its way through.
Much farther west, the stream's water, now increased a thousand times by other streams, emptied
into the Columbia River and eventually into the Pacific Ocean.

The canyon which would become Felis' home lay
in the eastern shadow of the Continental Divide.

Not that she deliberately chose the canyon—arrived there, looked it over and decided that this was
where she would stay. There was no decision made.
It all just happened.

Felis had crossed a high divide and was working
her way down the side of an especially rugged mountain. She heard a stream plunging among rocks far
below her. In her short life she had learned that
where there was water there were willows, and
where there were willows there might very well be
rabbits. Felis was hungry. On the lower slopes of the
mountain she reached an area which had been
burned over a few years earlier. It was a large, fifty-
acre patch of cleared land in the forest, with dead
trees lying like a pile of jackstraws. A new, second
growth was taking over—huckleberries, chokecherries, aspen, even some willows growing in the wet
earth. In fifty years or so it would be a fir forest again.
Felis turned aside and entered the clearing. There
might be rabbits here.

Then she saw the deer, an old doe, feeding on
aspen twigs. Felis dropped to her belly. The deer
hadn't sensed her yet. The cat squirmed forward,
froze when the deer looked up, then moved forward
again until she was within striking range. It was the
first time she had hunted so large an animal, yet she
instinctively knew what to do. She set her hind feet
for the charge. The black tip of her tail twitched back
and forth. The deer edged closer. When she was fifty
feet away, Felis charged. The old doe never knew
what had hit her. She dropped in her tracks and Felis
killed her with one powerful bite into her spine,
finishing with a death grip on the deer's throat. Her
first successful deer hunt. She draped the carcass
over her shoulder and dragged it out of the tangled
mess of downed trees. At the edge of the clearing she
opened the belly with her claws and disemboweled
it as she had seen her mother do. She dragged the
stomach and intestines aside so that the half-digested
food and acids they contained would not taint the
meat. Then she ate the heart, liver and lungs. After-
ward, she covered the carcass with a pile of dirt and

leaves, as cougars usually do with their kills. The pile would protect the meat from flies. Although Felis would return to the deer carcass until all the meat was eaten, she had no desire to eat rotten food. After covering the carcass, she walked down to the stream to drink. She surprised a beaver at work on his dam. The beaver saw her and sounded the alarm. *SMACK!* His flat tail slapped like a rifle shot against the water. Then he was gone, down to the safety of his lodge.

After drinking from the pond, Felis worked her way back up the mountain, past her cached deer, and onto a large, flat boulder overlooking Burned Clearing. She stretched out and fell asleep.

In the morning she was awakened by human voices. She looked down into the clearing where her deer was hidden and saw a man and a boy investigating her catch. Felis watched as they tied up the dog which trailed along behind them. They worked in the clearing all morning cutting wood. Then, when the sun was at its high point, the two humans gathered up their jackets and tools. They untied the dog and led him from the clearing. The last Felis saw of them was as they rounded the beaver pond.

She slipped down the hill and investigated her deer. It was still intact; the odor of the humans was all around. She snarled, but with this, her second human contact, she was becoming used to the odor. She ripped away more meat from the deer, then covered the carcass and retreated back to the sun-warmed slab of rock where she slept away the rest of the day.

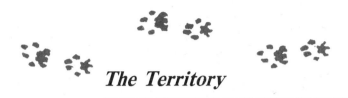

The Territory

The canyon proved to be a good home for Felis the cougar. It was rich in game—deer browsing in the little meadows and clearings, porcupines waddling through the forest, rabbits scurrying among the willows along the stream bed. High on the canyon's slopes there were boulders where Felis could lie sunning, and in the fir and pine forests there were trees where she could sharpen her claws and climb on the heavy branches to sprawl lazily in the warm summer afternoons.

The canyon was remote, far off the beaten track of man. Its only humans were the four people who lived downstream in the cabin. For the first week or so after Felis moved into the canyon the humans made her nervous. There was the odor of their wood smoke drifting up when the wind was just right. There were human sounds—the sharp crack of an axe as the man split firewood for winter; the noises of the boy and his sister playing; and, worst of all, the barking of the dog. She stayed well away from the people for many weeks after that first sighting of the man and boy in Burned Clearing. Sometimes at night she saw lights glowing in the windows of their cabin when she was out prowling her new home. One morning, she spotted laundry snapping in the breeze and was tempted to move in to investigate. But the dog began to bark, so she kept her distance.

Coyote (*Canis latrans*).

She had other neighbors, some of whom she saw often. Coyotes, for instance. On the morning after the incident in Burned Clearing, Felis returned to the deer carcass to feed. As she padded from the forest she saw a small, fawn-colored animal with long ears and a thin, pointed muzzle tearing meat from her deer. Her deer! Felis raised her head to make sure she actually saw what she thought she had seen; she cocked her ears, then bounded into the clearing after the intruder. The coyote heard her coming and scampered away, scrambling among the tangle of fallen trees, climbing up and over, completely outdistancing and eluding the heavier cougar. He disappeared into the forest. So Felis returned to the deer carcass. What she didn't know was that the coyote had run in a large circle which took him to a boulder overlooking the clearing. He stood there watching until Felis finished eating and had covered the carcass again. After she left, he slipped down the hill and resumed his interrupted meal.

She also heard the coyote and his friends, for they seemed to enjoy making each moonlit night come awake with their singing. *YIP! YIP! YIP, YIP, YIP, YIP, YIP!* Half a dozen coyotes calling back and forth across the canyon, ridge to ridge, as though saluting the full, round moon which climbed into the sky behind its screen of pine trees.

One evening Felis met another neighbor—a badger. She found him on a slope busily digging out a ground squirrel he had cornered in its burrow. The badger was a member of the weasel family. He had a stout, flattened body, a pointed snout, a long shaggy coat of gray and black fur with a white stripe that traveled the length of his back. He also had the most cantankerous disposition of any animal in the canyon. The badger brooked no nonsense from anyone, for life was a serious matter to him and each day was

Cougar and badger.
Ernest Wilkinson

Badger (*Taxidea taxus*),
cantankerous relative of
the weasel and otter.
San Diego Zoo

meant to be spent waddling ponderously about in search of rodents and other food. No time for curiosity about the world.

But Felis the cougar was of no such temperament. When she saw the badger's rear end sticking out of the burrow her first inclination was to investigate, to learn more about all of this. She approached carefully, ready to scamper away if the activity meant danger. But the badger was completely unaware of her, totally involved in digging his hole. Felis sat beside him, head cocked, watching. Her curiosity got the better of her; she cautiously reached out a paw and touched the badger's backside. Immediately, the scene changed. The badger whirled around and backed against the rear face of the burrow. His ears lowered against his head and he bared a row of wicked-looking teeth. Felis bounced back, then seeing that the badger wasn't going to come slashing out at her, slowly moved in. She batted gently at his head. He responded with a vicious swipe that missed the cougar's paw by a hairsbreadth. She circled him; tried to nip him and was rewarded by a painful bite on the chin. She drew away and sat watching.

With the immediate danger past, the badger returned to his digging, sending a shower of dirt from between his rear legs. It arched up and struck Felis on her face. She sneezed. The shower of dirt continued. The cougar lost patience with the badger and dashed in and grabbed him. But he was not to be held. He twisted inside his thick, loose coat, whirled and raked her with his long, sharp claws. Felis jumped back and pawed her torn cheek. She lunged again, thought better of it, and turned to bound down the hill. The badger, solid citizen that he was, resumed his digging.

Neither the badger nor the coyote posed a threat to Felis' safety. They, like the other animals living in the canyon, were merely parts of the wilderness and she accepted them as such, sometimes as nuisances, sometimes as objects to stimulate her tremendous curiosity, and, if she were hungry, as possible meals. The family of humans, however, were threats. At least she sensed they were. Her recent, nearly tragic experience with men had made her very cautious. However, since the family left her completely alone, gradually she came to accept them as part of the canyon's life.

Even if the people had tried to find her, they would have been disappointed. One of her first tasks in her new home was to seek out all its secrets, so she was constantly moving, seldom sleeping twice in the same place.

She found each little ravine that opened off the canyon, noting where rabbits lived among the willows and where the deer came down from the mountain for water. She walked the entire length of the stream, from the spring which gushed from under a boulder, several miles north to the meadow beyond the canyon's mouth where the stream joined with another. She nosed among the boulders that cluttered the slopes, and often found dens among them —the abandoned nurseries of coyotes and lynxes, the cave where a black bear had spent the previous winter. There was an eagle's nest, empty now except for bits of bones and fur of the little animals which the adult birds had brought back to their chicks. Hidden in a crevice between two boulders, Felis found a colony of wood rats, marked by a mass of twigs and leaves, fluff from the cottonwood trees, bits of glass and metal stolen from the cabin downstream, husks of pine nuts, brightly colored stones—anything which appealed to the little robber rats. The face of the boulder was stained with long, dark streaks—the leaching from the debris and rat droppings deposited in the nest above. Felis noted and recorded the location of the colony against the time of hunger which could strike deep in the long winter ahead. But for the time being, she left the rats alone. Hunting was good in the canyon, and after she finished off the deer carcass buried in Burned Clearing, she caught a few rabbits and porcupines, and a deer fawn.

She was very curious about the beavers and spent many hours watching them from her perch. The male beaver had come to the canyon three years earlier after being evicted from his parents' lodge farther upstream. He had been two years old then, sexually mature, and the time had come for him to leave home. So he set off to establish a place of his own, just as Felis had done later. He waddled downstream for several days until he came to the small meadow which lay at the head of the canyon. This, he knew instinctively, was an ideal place to establish a homesite. There was a year-round stream, plenty of cottonwood, aspen and willow trees for construction material and food, and there were no other beavers already in residence. The beaver set to work. First, he logged the trees near the place he chose for his dam. Some fell exactly right across the stream, but others went down at odd angles. These the beaver cut into pieces he could handle and dragged them out to the dam. Contrary to the folk tales about beavers, they are not expert loggers. They don't seem able to determine which way a tree will fall; they make anything but a clean cut; and often, they are pinned and killed by the very tree they are working on.

When his dam was finished and the pond full, the beaver began watching for any free female who might wander by. Eventually, one showed up, a young adult who had been forced to leave home by her parents. The two set up housekeeping and a new beaver family was begun.

Of all the animals in the canyon, the beaver was

the one which changed the environment most. When he cut trees to build his dam, he opened up the meadow and hillside to the sunlight, thus encouraging grass to grow. This drew deer and small rodents. When the dam was completed, the leakage across its length kept the land immediately downstream very wet, almost a marsh. Trees which had grown there for years died from drowning and remained as naked snags where hawks and eagles built nests. Thick stands of willows took root around the pond, providing food and shelter for rabbits and rodents. These small animals drew the predators—coyotes, lynxes, hawks and eagles. Finally, the beaver's dam served as a flood control device. Because of it, the stream no longer ran free, subject to heavy melting and other runoff. Its level stayed almost the same from springtime when the ice melted until the following autumn when everything froze.

So because of the dam—a barrier of tree trunks, branches, twigs, mud and grass—the upper end of the canyon was changed dramatically, and the entire watershed for miles downstream was influenced to some degree.

To maintain the dam, the beaver family worked constantly, plugging holes and strengthening weak places. And in between these chores, they gathered willow sprigs and aspen branches for food, often venturing far from the safety of the water in their quest.

Had they known they were being watched by Felis as they went about their work, they would have been far more careful than they were, and certainly would not have wandered from the pond. They, along with deer and porcupines, were the cougar's favorite food. But the cat kept her distance from them for the time being, content to merely study these neighbors. The deer supply was sufficient for her needs, and her prime concern—other than keeping her belly filled

—was to learn each corner of the country around Burned Clearing.

She wandered farther and farther afield as the weeks passed. And as she crossed and crisscrossed what was rapidly becoming her home territory, she sprayed trees, rocks and bushes, and built "scrapes" —piles of dirt and leaves covering her droppings. In effect, she was marking the boundaries of her territory; hanging "Keep Out" signs directed to other cougars.

The area she finally claimed was about twenty square miles in area, the average size of an adult cougar's home, so far as we know. Burned Clearing lay in its center, and the east and west boundaries ran along the crests of the hills bordering the canyon. The canyon's mouth was the territory's southern border and an abandoned prospector's cabin a few miles upstream more or less marked its northern edge.

She did not confine her wanderings to this "homesite." Like all cougars, she must hunt in order to live, and rich as the canyon was in game, it couldn't possibly support her. She traveled farther, into what would become her "hunting range." This was open territory and might be shared with other cougars. It included the mountain ridge to the east, in the direction of the lake where Felis had contacted the old female and her cubs. The farther she moved from her canyon, the more cautious she became, for as all territorial animals, Felis felt most comfortable within her own, clearly defined home. One morning she saw the old female and her cubs, and she circled to avoid them. Another day she spotted a big male eating a deer. She spent the afternoon watching him from the safety of a ledge. On still another occasion when she had wandered twenty miles from home, she came on a cougar scrape. It had been made by the big male. Felis sniffed it, then retraced her path, for the mark

Cougar and deer herd—predator and prey.

meant that she had invaded the male's territory, and instinctively Felis realized that she had no business there.

In this way, and over the first few weeks of her taking up residence in the canyon, Felis established her home territory, learned what was neutral ground and what areas were already occupied and claimed by other cougars. She often traveled as much as twenty miles in one night, padding through the forest and along watercourses by the light of the moon. If any human had been there to see her, she would have seemed to be a ghost slipping through the wilderness night.

The end of each of her lengthy circuits found her back home on the flat rock above Burned Clearing. In the mornings and evenings, deer moved into the clearing. They came timidly, nosing the air for danger before venturing from the safety of the forest. Then, one step at a time, like a swimmer trying the water with his toe before going in, they entered the clearing to nibble on aspen shoots, flicking their tails, wiggling their ears, constantly looking up to check for danger.

Felis seemed to enjoy watching the deer. If she were full she would lie on her rock for hours, out of sight, lazily observing the deer as they fed. But if she were hungry, it was another matter.

One night in late September she arrived back at her boulder after the moon had set. She was tired and hungry after a long walk across the sharp granite talus that lay below the crest. She flopped on the boulder and fell asleep. In the morning the sound of a twig snapping woke her. A deer was entering Burned Clearing. He was a fine six-year-old buck with a rack of antlers which gleamed like old pewter in the soft, gray light.

Felis snapped alert. She watched the buck's every movement as he walked carefully into the burn, searched for danger, then settled down to feed. Felis backed very slowly off the rock and dropped to the ground. She trotted down to the clearing, stopped at the edge and raised her head. The buck was several hundred feet away, working toward the clearing's center as he snipped away the aspen shoots. Felis retraced her path until she was out of sight of the clearing, then bounded through the trees to get closer to the buck. She stopped and peered through the trees. The buck was still feeding and now was directly across a narrow screening of pines from her. She inched forward. At the edge of the clearing she stopped again and looked. The buck had drifted farther into the clearing. Still out of range. Felis crept from the trees and slowly worked her way into the clearing, keeping a fallen log between herself and the deer. She peeked under the log and saw the buck's legs beyond. She couldn't possibly charge under the log, so she set her rear legs and jumped onto the log, planning to leap to the ground on the other side and dash the few yards that would separate her from her breakfast. But in leaping onto the log she dislodged a piece of bark which clattered to the ground. The buck whirled, saw the cougar and bounded farther into the clutter of fallen trees. Short, stiff-legged leaps, as though his legs were coiled springs. Felis jumped from the log and raced after the deer, leaping from log to log. The buck swung to the right, uphill. Felis cut across the circle he had taken. The buck left the clearing, but in his terror to escape he made a mistake. He ran into the pile of boulders which flanked the clearing's upper side. He was cut off. Felis closed in for the kill. Then the unexpected happened.

The buck wheeled around to face his pursuer. He

lowered his head and swung the awesome rack of antlers, honed to a fine edge in anticipation of fights with other bucks in the breeding season which lay ahead.

Felis drew up short. Then the buck actually charged her! She scurried away, perplexed. This had never happened to her before. The prey attacking the predator? Again the buck whirled, lowered his head and charged. Felis bounced back. She sat and cocked her head as though assessing this new turn of events. But the buck didn't let her sit for long. He came at her again, swinging his antlers and rearing onto his hind feet in order to slash with his razor-sharp front hoofs. He forced Felis back into the tangled mess of logs in Burned Clearing, backed her against a log, came directly at her, head lowered, antlers pointing at her body. She saved herself only by leaping straight into the air, clawing for a grip on the log and dashing away. Other arrangements would have to be made for breakfast that day.

In her dealings with the deer buck she discovered what all predators must learn very early in life if they are to survive. There are many, many failures on the hunt, far more than there are successes. A wolf pack, for instance, must attack an average of thirteen moose before killing one. In Felis' life, her degree of success would depend on several things—how well she concealed herself, how close the prey came to her place of concealment, how fast and accurately she charged, and what animals she chose to hunt. This last factor would prove to be very important and, as she perfected her hunting, Felis would recognize and avoid healthy, mature animals, especially the bucks, and concentrate on easier prey—fawns and diseased or old adults. This is how it has been for millions of years.

For as far back in time as we can search, we find

them living together—the predator and the animal on which he preys. Nothing lives alone, and life survives by feeding on itself. The hunter and the hunted live side by side as though they were links in a living chain—a food chain.

And that is what scientists call the predator/prey relationships—food chains. Some are simple; others are very complex. All have one thing in common: they begin with the sun.

Perhaps it seems strange to realize that the sun, which we take so much for granted, is so very important. But if there were no sunshine, there would be no plants, and without plants, there would be no animals. So, without sunshine no life on earth, at least no life as we know it.

A plant uses sunshine to convert water and carbon dioxide into food—sugar and starches—which the plant needs. It does this by a process called photosynthesis, and by using one of the plant's chemicals—chlorophyll. It is chlorophyll which makes plants green. So each leaf is a tiny factory, turning water and carbon dioxide into food.

Any factory produces waste products and the plants are no exception. Their waste is water and oxygen. Oxygen is one of the substances which all animals need in order to live. And one of the animals' waste products is carbon dioxide which the plants need. So each organism's waste is vital to the survival of the other.

Plants are extremely important to animals in another way. They are the basic food without which animals could not live. Animals must have organic food and plants are the only organisms capable of converting inorganic material into organic compounds. Thus, the life-giving energy of the sun eventually finds its way into the belly of an animal.

Herbivores—those animals which eat vegetation—

consume the excess foliage which plants produce, and, in this way, take in some of the sun's energy. These animals which live by eating plants are called first order consumers.

Predators, such as the cougar, eat the herbivores, and in this way they too participate in the sun's energy. The predator which eats the herbivore is called a second order consumer.

Man is a part of many food chains. The simplest is when he acts as a first order consumer by eating vegetables. Plant and man—two links. A bit more complex chain occurs when man eats beef. He is then a second order consumer eating an animal which lived by eating plants. An example of an even more complicated food chain would be the following: man eats a tuna fish, which lived on smaller fish, which ate still smaller fish, which ate the tiny ocean animals called plankton. The plankton, in turn, ate microscopic plants called phytoplankton—a six-link chain. In each of these chains, man is the ultimate consumer, that is, he is at the end of the food chain, for nothing feeds on him. The same thing is true of the other large predators—lions, wolves, hawks, eagles, and so forth. All are ultimate consumers.

But it is not completely true that nothing feeds on them. After these ultimate consumers die, they are attacked by a host of microscopic animals—bacteria —which decompose their bodies back into the chemicals and minerals of which they are made. These are used by the plants as part of their food, and the food chain starts all over again.

So this chain of life does not run in a straight line —beginning to end. Life goes on and on, feeding on itself and constantly drawing energy from the sun.

A food chain is possible only because nature is very extravagant, producing more of everything than is needed. There are many times more phytoplankton than needed to feed the plankton. (It is interesting to note here that these tiny, microscopic plants produce seventy-five per cent of the world's oxygen.) There are many more plankton than required and more fish eggs than will become adult fish. Throughout the whole of life, there are more babies born than will live to adulthood.

The reason for this enormous overproduction is the high mortality—the death rate—of life, especially wilderness life. Most wilderness babies, fish, bird and mammal, die long before they grow up.

One of the main hazards they face is presented by the food chain itself. The killing goes on day and night, taking a heavy toll. And the lower on the food chain we look, the greater that toll is. Each time the sun's energy is passed along—from plant to animal and from one animal to another—some of the original energy is lost. So each consumer on the chain must eat more than the one which came before him. In this sense, the "chain" might be best pictured as a food "pyramid" with astronomical numbers of first order consumers—plankton, for instance—needed to support a high order consumer—a man, in this case.

Tragic as the killing is for the individual animals who are caught, it is extremely important for the well-being of the prey species as a whole. Since the weakest animals are the ones taken—the very young, very old and diseased—the best are left to reproduce the species. Old animals which can no longer reproduce are of no use to the herd. They simply eat food needed by younger, more vigorous individuals and the herd is better off without them. Diseased animals who fall to predators are kept from spreading their illness. And the young which are caught are the slowest or least intelligent or crippled or whatever it is that keeps them from being the absolute best of the new crop of babies. Since nature is unforgiving, they must go. So the food chain not only provides food for predators, it also acts to cull out those individuals which weaken the prey species.

Predators tend to specialize in the types of animals they hunt. Usually this is determined by the hunter's size. Foxes, lynxes, weasels, and the predator birds hunt small rodents since they can't kill big animals. The large carnivores—wolves and cougars in North America—concentrate on deer, moose and elk. Mountain people claim that where you find deer, you'll also find cougar.

That was the main reason that Felis chose the canyon as her home, that and the fact there was no other cougar already there. If there had been no deer, she would have continued drifting, seeking a place that was rich in her favorite food. Of course she ate other animals—rabbits, porcupines and other rodents— but she was young and unskilled as a hunter. As she mastered the hunting craft she would rely less and less on small animals when deer were available. After all, hunting was hard work, whether the prey was a deer or a rabbit. Why not hunt the one with the most meat? So, for the rest of her life, she would remain tied to deer. If they moved, she would go along with them.

That is exactly what happened four months after she came to the canyon.

By late September, the first hints of autumn came to Burned Clearing where summer's heat was dissipated early in the thin mountain air. The huckleberries ripened and were harvested by birds and the black bear who lived on the opposite side of the canyon. One day, the human family trudged up to the clearing to gather berries. They worked on their knees, combing the tiny red huckleberries off the low-growing bushes. When they had filled several

San Diego Zoo

Elk (*Cervus canadensis*). This zoo-raised
individual is bugling—a call which can be
related to sexual courtship.

one-gallon cans, they walked back down the mountain. Felis retired high onto the ridge while they
were in the clearing.

The quaking aspen leaves began to change from
the dark, dusty green of late summer to brilliant gold.
Pine cones ripened and scattered their seeds across
the clearing, and the chipmunks and jays came to
harvest them. The grasses headed out and dried,
keeping hundreds of field mice busy gathering food
for the winter which lay just around the corner. By
day, the mice were preyed on by hawks who rode the
air currents high above Burned Clearing, watching
for a mouse who left his runway. And in the clear,
cold nights, the mice fell to the great horned owls
who swooped down on silent wings and scooped up
the rodents before they knew that danger was near.

In those early days of autumn, the rutting season
came on the deer and elk. It was time to conceive the
babies which would be born the following spring.
High in the mountain meadows where the does gathered in small groups and ate the last of the season's
grasses, the males moved in to claim harems. They
fought with rivals, fencing with their new, hard antlers and rearing onto their hind legs to slash with the
sharp front hoofs. Now and then, a pair of bucks
became locked together when their antlers tangled,
and unless they were able to break loose, they stayed
together until both of them died, either from starvation or beneath the claws of a predator. The clear,
bold bugling call of bull elks came from far back in
the mountains, echoing down the canyon in the
crisp, clear air. The rut lasted for several weeks then
faded away. The does moved in small groups as they
usually did, and the males drifted away for another
year.

By mid-October, each clearing on the mountainsides seemed filled with shimmering golden bouquets, bursts of color splashed against the somber, dark green backgrounds of pine and fir. The aspen had turned color. Willows along the watercourses glowed deep, blood red. The wild rose bushes growing on the lower slopes weathered to a rich brown. Each morning, the grass and bushes were glazed by frozen dew which melted away by nine or ten o'clock. During the warmth of the afternoons, the lazy humming of the season's last insects filled the air. The year was dying.

One night a small storm drifted across the mountains. The canyon awoke the following morning to a white, silent world in which each bush and tree was powdered with a thin covering of snow. The rabbits, caught before their coats had completely changed for winter, huddled among the bare willows, mottled brown and white, easy targets for any predator. A flight of sparrows winged down the canyon, bound for warmer climates. They already had been replaced by juncos which arrived earlier from the north. These little brown birds with the black hoods over their heads and shoulders would stay for a month or so, until the temperature dropped much lower. Then they too would seek a more mild wintering ground. The eagles and hawks were gone, settled in the lower valleys for the winter. Of the predatory birds, only the owls would winter in the high mountains.

The annual migration of birds has always fascinated man. He has seen them come from the north in autumn, spend just a few days in his area or perhaps even the entire winter. Then in spring, they fly back to their northern breeding grounds. Yet it has been only recently that man has understood the mechanisms which trigger these enormous journeys. For thousands of years, he assumed that it was the temperature that sent hundreds of thousands of birds flying away. After all, they came south for winter, which would logically mean that they left the north when the weather became too cold. And in spring, when the weather warmed, they flew north again. Recent studies indicate that the birds respond, not so much to temperature as to light. The migrating birds are one of many species of animals which have biological "light clocks" inside their bodies. They seem to have special cells which are sensitive to the light —its amount and duration. And when the sunlight decreases to a certain point, that is, when the days become shorter, these light clocks trigger the drive to migrate south. By the same token, when the daylight lengthens, the birds return north.

By noon of the day of that first storm the thin covering of snow had melted from the lower slopes of the canyon's wall, and the deer and elk returned to the clearings to feed. They were gorging now, building up layers of fat on their bodies to carry them into winter. The black bear was stuffing herself with berries, fish, the meat left by Felis and the other hunters—anything that was edible. Soon she would retreat into her cave to sleep until spring. The canyon's creatures were preparing for cold weather.

It came in early November, riding a wild storm that screamed down the canyon. The temperature fell to five degrees above zero. Swirling masses of snow whipped through the trees and piled in deep drifts on the lee sides of the boulders. It blanketed the willows, bending them to the ground. It crushed the grass runways of the field mice. It swirled and eddied around the entrance to the bear's cave, sealing it for the winter. It buried the trails that deer and elk had made on their way to the stream. And when the storm finally died, snow lay more than two feet deep throughout the canyon. The sky cleared, and the temperature plummeted to below zero. The stream froze over, the beaver pond at the upper end of the canyon disappeared under a covering of ice, and only the mound of snow at its lower end marked the site of the beaver's lodge.

After that first massive storm, the deer moved down from the high country. They had gone to the clearings for feed, but the clearings were covered by deep snow. One by one, or in small groups, they worked their way to spots on the canyon's floor where the storm had not struck with such ferocity. So Felis the cougar left her flat rock overlooking Burned Clearing.

The coming of winter meant little to her. Her coat was thick and heavy, protecting her from the cold. And, unlike the herbiverous animals, she did not have to store up food for winter, for her food supply was always nearby. So long as there were deer or hares or porcupines, she would eat. But she had to stay close to them. When the storm drove the deer from the canyon's upper slopes, Felis shifted her range to coincide with theirs. Its center for the winter would be close to the mouth of the canyon and the narrow road which led to the settlement.

Thus it was that she discovered the boy. During the late summer and autumn the humans had stayed away from Burned Clearing except for the two times when they cut firewood and gathered huckleberries. Their cabin was downstream and the little placer mine they worked was even farther away. So Felis had little to do with them. But when she moved off the slope she accidentally took up residence close to the trail which the boy used in walking to school each day.

She was lying in the shelter of a boulder one morning when she heard him coming down the trail. *Shu-ush, shuush,* through the snow. He was alone, for his half-Airedale, half-wolf dog was not allowed to follow him to school. One of the families which lived at the settlement kept chickens and the dog loved to chase them. Because the chickens' owner threatened to shoot the dog if he chased the chickens again, the family wisely kept him near the cabin.

When Felis heard the boy shuffling through the snow she raised her head to learn the source of the sound. But a screening of pines blocked her view. The sound drew closer, passed by and faded away. Felis rose and walked cautiously through the trees. There, in the trail, were the boy's footprints. Felis sniffed. The odor hanging in the air was human, but not the same as the horrifying smell she remembered from that day when she was fired on. This was a mixture of rubber galoshes, corduroy pants, a sheepskin coat, books, mittens and the odds and ends that a boy carries in his pockets. Felis was curious. She followed the footprints beyond the canyon, across the stream and up the hill on the other side. At one point she almost came on the boy, who had stopped to study a snowshoe rabbit's trail. She bounced into the forest and sat watching him. He was the same kind of creature who had shot at her, no doubt about that. He walked on his rear legs and used his front legs to carry a lunch box and books. He had the same round head as those other creatures. But there was something different about him. In the first place, he was much smaller, so small that Felis sensed no danger from him. There was no dog with him, neither did he carry a gun. So when he straightened up from the rabbit's tracks and continued walking, Felis moved back onto his trail and followed. She sniffed at the rabbit's tracks. Nothing interesting there. The trail was cold and the rabbit which had made it might be far away. But the boy's trail was fresh and different from anything Felis had ever encountered. She followed him for another mile until she heard dogs

barking in the village. Then she turned aside and
trotted into the woods. She wanted nothing to do
with dogs.

The country was new to the cat for she had
confined her wanderings north and east of the canyon, avoiding the more populated area near the settlement. Now she walked deeper into the forest and
climbed the hill which overlooked the village. At the
top she stood on a boulder surveying the scene below. The village lay half a mile to the west. Felis saw
the boy she had followed run down the hill and min-
gle with other children. She saw smoke coming from
the few houses and the stone school. A pair of railroad tracks passed through the settlement and
swung around the base of the hill on which Felis
stood. Several men in the village pushed a small car
onto the tracks, started an engine and putt-putted off
to work on the tracks.

There was a ranch lying at the base of the hill,
small, a mere clearing in the forest, with a log cabin
house, a pole barn and a few acres of pasture. Two
horses nosed the snow in the pasture, looking for a bit
of grass. Felis had never seen a horse before. She
lowered herself onto the boulder and sat watching
them until a gnarled little man came out in mid-
morning to care for them. From her great distance,
Felis didn't recognize him as one of the men who had
ambushed her that day in the meadow.

She followed the boy several times that autumn,
each time ending up lying on the flat boulder above
the ranch.

As November faded into December a new, strange
desire arose inside her. She was two years old, a
young adult, and she was beginning to feel the need
of a mate. She became nervous and irritable, yet she
had no object against which to launch her frustra-
tions. She roamed deep into the territory of the male

cougar which lived near the lake. She sought out his scrapes and the places where he had scratched tree trunks. She rubbed against the markings he had left on bushes and boulders. And she trotted nervously for hours through the forest, mewing low, deep-throated sounds, calling for a mate. One night in late December, she raised her voice in a scream. It was a wild cry that rose high into the upper register, hung there in the frozen air, silencing the other sounds of the canyon. It echoed back and forth from the boulders, and sent the tiny mice scurrying for the safety of their burrows. Then it faded and was gone. There is no way to know whether Felis was calling for the mate she so desperately wanted or was actually greeting him. In either case, the male from the adjoining territory had caught the scent she left behind when she rubbed against his markings. He followed the trail she left and found her in her territory. After staying with her for two weeks he moved back across the mountain into his own home range. He would contribute nothing to the care and feeding of the cubs he had sired. In fact, if he ever encountered them, he might try to kill them.

Her brief honeymoon over, Felis returned to the life she had known before the mating urge gripped her. She spent each day hunting, eating, sleeping or following the boy to school. As the winter deepened, hunting took more and more of her time, for the heavy snow made her short, high-speed dashes all but impossible and the vast majority of her would-be victims escaped. Yet she still had to eat, so she spent many hours working at her craft—spotting and identifying a victim, creeping as close as possible to it, lying in ambush, then charging in a fast, perfectly coordinated drive.

The Winter

With the passing of the old year, winter took over absolute control of the canyon, gripping it in a merciless, frozen fist. Daylight hours were short and cold, nights even colder. The temperature dropped to thirty degrees below zero and stayed there. Day after day the sky was covered by a somber, charcoal-gray blanket of clouds, heavy with snow. Storms screamed out of the north, one on the heels of the other, each seeming to be more ferocious than the last. In the short interludes between them, a deathly stillness hung over the canyon, broken only by the sound of snow sloughing from an overloaded fir tree, or the sharp crack of an axe as the man of the human family split firewood. Bluish-gray wood smoke from the cabin's fireplace hung in the air, sending its wispy tendrils snaking among the trees and curling slowly over the snow-covered boulders. Each morning, the man would start the placer mine pump engine. *PUTT—PUTT—PUTT.* The sound reverberated the length of the leafless, grassless, snow-buried canyon. And each morning, the boy would shuffle along his trail, bound for school.

Felis the cougar had a favorite spot among a pile of boulders from which to watch the boy pass by without being seen. And once or twice a week, if her stomach were full, she would swing onto the trail and

follow him, always turning away at the same place—
the brow of the hill overlooking the village—and
wending her way to the boulder overlooking the
ranch. During the coldest weather the horses were
kept inside their barn, and Felis saw only the ranch
owner, bundled up as he went about his chores, his
head wreathed in a cloud of frozen breath.

For the most part, the cougar had very little time
to follow the boy or lie watching the ranch. The cubs
developing inside her body needed nourishment.
She must hunt. Winter proved to be a mixed blessing
—although the deep snow made the cougar's style of
hunting more difficult, it also worked to the deers'
disadvantage by forcing them to bunch up, thus becoming more vulnerable. They sought sheltered
areas where they could paw through the snow for
grass and reach up to strip twigs from the trees. At
best, the deer seemed to have made a poor adapta-
tion to the bitterly cold weather which came to the
mountains.

Each of the canyon's other creatures had developed its own way to face winter. The adaptations had
been long in evolving—thousands of years—and not
all had been successful. Changes had been forced on
the animals very rapidly in evolutionary terms, beginning about one million years ago with the coming
of the first ice age. Enormous glaciers inched out of
the Arctic and covered much of the northern hemisphere. The land lay frozen for centuries. Life had to
change or die. The ice came and withdrew four
times. We are living in the final moments, geologi-
cally, of the latest withdrawal. Each time the ice ad-
vanced, a few more species of animals became
extinct, perhaps because they were unable to adjust
to the extreme conditions. The sabretoothed tiger,
the Dire wolf, Irish elk, woolly mammoth and the
mastodon are just a few which disappeared.

Those who survived developed many survival techniques. Today, some animals, especially birds, simply leave when winter approaches. They move to warmer climates. Other animals stay in their homeland but spend the winter indoors. The beaver, for instance, remains in his lodge during the cold weather, eating the twigs and branches he had the foresight to store up during summer. The beaver's lodge is a pile of brush located in his pond. Its entrance is below water and the lodge itself projects above the waterline. Because the lodge is surrounded by water, the beaver is safe from predators. And because its entrance is well below the surface, he can come and go when the pond is frozen. During the summer, the beaver does little but sleep, eat and work. Mainly work. He cuts trees to keep his dam in repair and as a supply of food for winter. He carries twigs and small branches to the bottom of the pond and drives them into the mud. Then, when the outside world is frozen and covered by snow, he draws on this food supply to last him for the winter.

Other animals also stay indoors all winter, but, unlike the beaver, they sleep. Many actually hibernate. That is, through a process we do not fully understand, their bodily functions—heartbeat, respiration, etc.—slow almost to the point of death. Because there is little need for nourishment during hibernation, the animals can live off the fat they accumulated during summer. Many rodents which live in cold climates hibernate. So do reptiles and amphibians— snakes, lizards, frogs and toads—the cold-blooded animals. Their body temperatures are the same as that of the surrounding air. As winter approaches and the temperature of the air drops, so does the body temperature of the cold-blooded animals. They become lethargic. Frogs burrow into the mud of their pond; snakes slip into burrows; lizards find crevices in the rocks. All those of the northlands spend the winter hibernating, completely unconscious of the cold weather.

Some mammals, notably bears, do not actually hibernate, but fall into a deep sleep, the difference being the rate at which their bodily functions perform. Bears store up vast reserves of fat before retiring for the winter, and they emerge in spring, thin and ravenously hungry.

Many animals neither migrate nor hibernate for the winter but face it head on, awake and active. Some, such as wolves, grow thick undercoats to insulate themselves from the cold. Certain prey species need protection not only from the cold but from predators as well. One of the most dramatic means they use is to change color; they become as invisible as possible. Snowshoe rabbits change from brownish gray to white as winter approaches. So do the Arctic birds called ptarmigans. And at least one species of predator—the weasel—undergoes the same change. In summer, a northland weasel is dark brown; when winter approaches they become pure white and then are called ermine. The process of using body color as camouflage is called "protective coloration," and is found throughout the animal world. Those animals which live in the desert, for instance, tend to be sandy colored. Certain snakes which live on the floor of the jungle forests are mottled and blend with the pattern of the leaves which clutter the ground. Many marine animals are dark on their backs and light on the bellies. When seen from above they blend in with the dark water; seen from beneath they disappear against the light undersurface of the sea. Sometimes, nature provides protective coloration for just part of an animal's life when it is most needed. The babies of many species are spotted or striped or otherwise marked to blend with the background. Then, as they

grow, the markings change to the adult patterns.
Deer fawns are an example of this. The babies are not
only spotted, which makes them very difficult to see
in the forest with its dappled light, they are also without scent. That is, they do not have a distinctive deer
odor. If they lie still, they can be safe from a predator
even when it approaches within a few feet.

But as adults, deer do little to adapt to the extremes of their environment, especially to winter.
True, they eat heavily in summer and autumn, building up layers of fat to help see them through. But it
isn't enough, and they must forage even when the
snow is deepest and the weather the most severe. So
they move from the high country and bunch up in
sheltered spots.

Felis the cougar discovered early in the winter
where the canyon's deer wintered. One area was at
the mouth of the canyon where a thick growth of
willows provided browse material and where the
snow did not drift to impossible depths. Another was
a quarter of a mile away on a southern slope in the
lee of a hill where grass grew heavily and the deer
could paw away the snow to reach it. The canyon's
summer range easily supported its fifty or sixty deer
which were scattered along both slopes and on the
crests. But during winter these animals congregated
in the two sheltered areas, making too heavy a de-
mand on the vegetation. The population was too
large for the carrying capacity of the winter range.
Unless the number was reduced, many deer would
starve before spring. In this regard, Felis was an important member of the natural process.

One morning, after trailing the boy and lying for
an hour on the boulder above the ranch, she became
aware of a gnawing in her stomach. Dinnertime. She
retraced her path back to the canyon's mouth, where
she circled the area where the deer were feeding. As

she neared them her pace slowed, and she dropped close to the ground. On a rise at the edge of the clearing she dropped flat, head raised, scanning the dozen or so deer that were pawing through the snow. She spotted a buck off to one side, stripping bark from a growth of willows. The buck was a "gummer," an old animal whose teeth were worn away. He was badly undernourished. The internal parasites which all deer have and which under normal conditions do not bother them, had further weakened him. Felis knew, with the special wisdom that wild predators have, that he was an easy target. The other healthier and younger members of the herd were passed over. The old buck was her prey.

She moved in slowly until she was close to him. She settled into the snow and squirmed her rump, setting her rear legs for the charge. Then, when the buck was within range, she attacked, swiftly and silently, her eyes fixed on the deer. When she reached him, she reared up and fastened her claws in his shoulder. The deer toppled over.

The rest of the herd dashed away when she came charging into the clearing. Some went farther up the hill, others crossed the stream and ran into the second feeding area. Felis had forced them to scatter, to use their entire winter range rather than just one part of it. In this way, she helped keep the range from being overeaten.

She also helped in another way. By killing the old buck, which was no longer a vital, reproducing member of the herd, she had assured that there would be more food for the other members.

During her attack, Felis did not make a sound. That would have been stupid, and merely warned the deer. She did not hate the deer, nor did she love killing it. To her, the deer was a meal, nothing more, and the hunt was the only way she had of getting the

A cougar whose attention is caught by
something presents a picture of concentration
—eyes alert and fixed, ears cocked forward.

meal. Her eyes didn't blaze nor her face contort in a bloodthirsty lust during her charge. She watched the deer carefully, but she was impassive, alert, efficient—a craftsman practicing its craft. And, despite what many humans say about cougars, she was not bloodthirsty. She did not kill for sport, as humans do, nor in rage, nor for spite. She killed clean and quickly as nature had adapted her to do, and for one reason only—to eat.

And the deer? What about him, the victim? Did he suffer for long? Many authorities on animal behavior claim that prey animals probably feel no pain or at the most, for only a split second. These people think that the shock of being attacked paralyzes the prey animal, making it numb to pain.

After making her kill, Felis hoisted the buck onto her back and half-dragged, half-carried it through the deep snow to a protected spot under the trees. There she disemboweled it and satisfied her hunger. Then she buried the carcass under snow and brush. She sat washing her face, and then ambled back to her favorite loafing spot near the boy's trail. The deer still were scattered, feeding along the entire length of the meadow. It would be several days before they concentrated again in the willow area.

By February, the very young and very old deer and those weakened by disease had been cropped from the herd, either by starvation or Felis' hunting. Those who remained became harder to get, and for each deer the cougar succeeded in killing, she missed a dozen others. Her periods of hunger became longer. Yet the cubs developing in her body would not be denied. She spent all her waking hours in search of food. One night, after a week of failure, she was traveling up the canyon in search of rabbits. Suddenly she stopped and tested the air. There was no mistaking the smell drifting down to her. Deer meat.

Felis licked her chops. She turned aside from the rabbit hunt to track down that tantalizing odor. It grew stronger. Felis broke into a trot, then a lope. Now it was very close. She broke through the willows lining the stream. She was less than one hundred feet from the humans' cabin. The smell was coming from there. Felis stopped and sat back to study this turn of events. Aside from trailing the boy, she had stayed well away from the canyon's humans, wanting nothing to do with them. Now, it seemed, they had something she wanted very badly. The odor of the deer meat made her salivate. But to be so close to humans! She partially rose and backed slowly into the willows. The odor followed. She sat and looked at the cabin. A soft glow of light from a kerosene lamp inside flickered against the frosted windows and cast little patches of light on the snow. A slender plume of wood smoke drifted from the fireplace chimney. Outside, nothing moved. Felis took one careful step forward. Nothing happened. Another step. Still nothing. Slowly, and very cautiously, she approached the cabin. She brushed the wild rose bush growing at the edge of the yard. The bush's load of snow sloughed onto her back. Felis leaped aside and raced up the hill. Nothing screamed or yelled or chased her. She stopped and looked down on the cabin roof. The odor of deer meat was even stronger up here. She inched toward the cabin. At its far end, a snowdrift reached almost to the roof. Felis walked to the edge of the drift and leaned forward, stretching as far as possible to savor the fragrance of the meat. Finally, unable to resist, she leaped lightly to the roof and walked toward a ventilator sticking up through the snow. It was directly above the root cellar and the deer was hanging inside. *CREAK. CREAK.* The roof sagged under her, but now she was aware only of the meat that was so near at hand. *CREAK.*

Suddenly, pandemonium broke loose inside the cabin. The dog! His frenzied barking came up to her, and panic struck the cougar. She wheeled around and bounded the length of the roof, leaped far out onto the snowbank and dashed for the safety of the willows. Great, ten-foot-long leaps. Doubling her body for leverage in the snow, then stretching far out to put as much distance as possible between her and the cabin. Ten minutes later, wheezing from exhaustion, she gained the safety of her niche at the mouth of the canyon.

The winter dragged on. Still another storm added more snow to the four-foot-deep pack already on the ground. Now, in the depth of winter, the animals of the canyon suffered terribly from the cold and hunger. Wilderness creatures do not experience winter as humans do. To them it is not a time of frozen beauty and outdoor sports with a warm fire to come home to. Winter is the time of hunger. Snow buries the grass and makes travel from one sheltered area to another almost impossible. The deer beat out yards where there is browse hanging on the trees. As the cold weather hangs on they gradually eat anything they can reach, even fir needles and old twigs. They grow thin and gaunt and many die of starvation. Only the strong survive until spring. But they are the most important individuals to the herds, for they become the parents of the next generation.

In a hard winter, even the animals which are best adapted to the cold suffer. Little buntings—snowbirds—often fall during a severe storm. They huddle together, feathers fluffed out to protect them from the cold. Then when the storm breaks, many lie frozen on the ground. Insect eggs, lying dormant in their cases in the crevices of trees or buried under the duff on the forest floor, are frozen solid. Hibernating reptiles freeze to death in their dens. Even the carnivores, from tiny ermine to the wolves and cougar, grow thin as the food supply disappears.

For Felis, the winter was doubly hard because of the unborn cubs. By the last of February they were just one month away from birth and required massive amounts of nourishment.

They had begun life more than two months earlier, in December, as tiny eggs, each no larger than the period at the end of this sentence. When the eggs, called ova, were fertilized by the male cougar, they fastened onto the wall of Felis' uterus—her womb— where each of them would stay until the cub developing from it was ready to be born. A water-filled sac formed around each cub which was called a fetus at this stage of development. The purpose of the sac was to cushion the fetus from shock as its mother went about her life, running, jumping, hunting. The fetus received nourishment through a cord—the umbilical cord—which connected it to the placenta, a spongy lining on the uterus. The nourishment came from Felis' bloodstream and the food she ate. It passed through the placenta's extremely thin walls, into the umbilical cord, and then into the fetus' bloodstream. A certain amount of the cubs' waste passed back along the umbilical cord, through the placenta and into Felis' system where it was disposed of. The cord which attached the cubs to their mother was truly a lifeline.

During the ninety days they spent inside their mother's body, the cubs grew faster than they ever would again in the same amount of time. In just three months they developed from tiny eggs to little ten-inch-long animals which weighed almost one pound each at birth. This period of their lives was known as gestation.

All placental animals—those with the spongy lining on their uteruses—have a gestation period. It varies from species to species. Usually, small animals have a shorter period than larger species. Mice, for instance, gestate for only about three weeks. At the other extreme, elephants have a twenty-one-month gestation period. For humans, it is normally two hundred and eighty days, roughly nine months.

The purpose of gestation is to provide a warm, safe place, well supplied with food, in which the unborn babies can develop. Mammals spend weeks or months inside their mothers' bodies, then are born live. Other animals, such as birds, insects and many reptiles and fish, develop inside eggs which the mothers lay. Most birds incubate their eggs, keeping them warm with their bodies. Insects, for the most part, merely deposit eggs on twigs or in the crevices of trees, or even underground, then move on, leaving the unborn babies to fend for themselves. Some fish protect their eggs. Others, such as the Pacific salmon, die immediately after laying and fertilizing the eggs.

Regardless of how each species starts life, the unborn babies get special attention from nature. If the eggs are to be left unprotected, tens of thousands of these eggs are laid to make sure some will hatch. If the babies are carried around inside their mothers' bodies, they are surrounded by the water-filled sac to protect them from injury. Nature is very caring of her unborn young. She must be, for this is the only way that life will survive.

But if she is protective of the generation still to be born, she seems overdemanding on its mothers. The babies must be fed, and in the case of carnivores, this means more prey must be killed. Because the cubs developing inside Felis would be born in spring, the cougar had to provide for the fetuses during the worst part of the year—winter.

As the deer became more difficult to bring down,

she turned to whatever animals she could find.
Hares, for instance. But even they made her work
hard for each meal. The big hares were beautifully
adapted for winter. First, they were white and almost impossible to see against the snow. And they
had long, powerful hind legs and feet, which supported them on the snow. Felis sank to her belly in
the deep snow, but the hares stayed on the surface,
and so could escape.

One morning she visited the rats' nest she had
discovered early in her habitation of the canyon.
Even the small rodents which she usually avoided
eating, seemed good now. But the canyon's other
predators also knew about the colony of rats.

Felis worked her way among the jumble of rocks
that protected the nest. The rats had built their home
on a ledge formed by two large boulders. It was ac-
cessible to large animals only through a narrow cleft
between the two rocks. Felis squeezed through the
cleft and approached the debris-strewn nest. She saw
that it extended back into a cave formed by the boulders. In the snow outside the cave she saw the marks
left by other animals—the tiny, precise prints of a
weasel, a coyote's tracks, an owl's feather. But there
was no sign of the rats. They had been eaten, or had
escaped to set up housekeeping elsewhere on the
mountain. The cougar searched the entire area, even
well back into the cave. She pawed through the debris on the floor—fir needles, the fluff from cottonwood trees, bits of metal and glass stolen from the
humans. Not one rat. Disgusted, she climbed back
through the cleft. But unconsciously, she filed the
memory of the cave for a future need.

To satisfy her hunger, she turned to still another
source of food—porcupine. There were many of
these slow, clumsy rodents in the canyon. In summer, they fed on buds and new shoots of the willows

Porcupine (*Erethizon ·dorsatum*). This quilled rodent is a relatively easy prey for cougars.

and small trees, and in winter they ate away the bark of the fir, pines and aspen. If they girdled a tree—ate away the bark completely around the trunk—the tree would die. There were many dead and dying trees in the canyon, the victims of porcupines.

But slow and clumsy though they were, porcupines posed problems for Felis for they were superbly defended by a coat of sharp quills across their backs and tails. The cougar had a special technique she used against them. It was one she had learned very early in life from watching her mother.

One cold night in late February while she was scouring the countryside for food, Felis heard the familiar grunting of a porcupine. She followed the sound and came upon the rodent as it sat in a fir tree, methodically gnawing away the bark. Normally, the cougar preferred to attack on the ground, but she was very hungry and wasn't inclined to wait for the porcupine to come down. So she dug her claws into the tree's trunk and clambered up to a branch growing at the same level as the one the porcupine sat on. The porcupine saw her and swung into its defensive position—rump facing the cougar, quills erect and tail swinging rapidly. One touch of that tail would load Felis' muzzle or paws with quills. Each was a tiny spear that could work its way into the victim's body and even kill if it punctured a vital organ. Contrary to folklore, the porcupine could not shoot her quills. They were simply hairs, modified to provide protection, and they were loosely attached to the skin. At the slightest touch, they fastened themselves in the victim. Felis had had many experiences with porcupines and knew the danger involved.

She swiped cautiously with a paw, then jerked it away as the porcupine swung its tail. She made a halfhearted snap at the porc's rump, then drew away. She sat back and cocked her head as though studying the situation. All of the porcupines she had killed thus far had been on the ground where the killing technique was fairly simple. It was just a matter of being fast, of thrusting a paw under the porcupine and flipping it onto its back where it lay helpless. Since there were no quills on the belly, one slash with the claws would kill the victim. But what to do when the would-be victim was firmly clamped to a tree branch and that deadly tail was in the way?

Felis swiped again with a paw and almost got hit with the tail. Very frustrating. She snarled. The porcupine sat impassively, tail swinging, quills erect. The cougar had to get around that tail. She moved along her branch and reached across to the porcupine's limb, well away from the spot where he was sitting. The limb bent beneath her. She put her other front paw on the limb and it bent even more. Felis leaped onto the branch. It was small, much too small to support the combined weight of the two animals. With a loud *CRACK,* the branch broke, sending cougar and porcupine tumbling amidst a flurry of fir and snow. Felis scrambled from under the branch and looked for the porcupine. He was already waddling away. But now there was no question about the outcome. Felis bounded up to him, and before the porcupine could even raise its quills, she had flipped him onto his back and killed him. Later that night, when the moon rose, she was back on her boulder near the deer yards, her belly filled again.

The time was rapidly approaching when a mere boulder would no longer be a proper home. Pleasant as it was to lie in the sun during the lengthening days, it would not provide the safety and protection needed for the cubs. So, between her hunting trips, the cougar looked for a place where she could bear and raise her family.

Nature's children are born under vastly different

conditions. For many, the moment of birth occurs with no parents or other protection at hand. For instance, the insects, fish and reptiles which hatch long after the parents have moved on or died. From the instant of hatching these young creatures are completely on their own. They must feed and protect themselves with no help. The mortality rate of these babies is awesome. For each one which survives to adulthood, hundreds and sometimes thousands have died. So it is vital that enough eggs be laid to assure that the species will continue. Other babies which also hatch from eggs are better protected. Most birds are excellent parents. They build nests, lay eggs, incubate them, then feed and care for the chicks, sometimes for months and, in a few cases, for years. As you would expect, a larger percentage of these babies live to maturity, so there is no need for a huge egg production. Most birds lay from three to a dozen, and there is one, the condor, which lays one or two eggs only every second year.

As a group, mammal babies are probably the best cared for of all nature's children. Because they are born alive rather than as eggs, they always have the mother with them. She takes care of their immediate needs and nurses them for weeks or months until they can feed themselves. And in many cases, she will fight to save them from predators.

But the conditions under which mammals are born also vary widely. The mammal we know best—man —comes into the world in antiseptic surroundings with a doctor or midwife in attendance. Then, for the next fifteen years or so he is fed, housed, clothed and loved by his parents. Wild animals which live in packs—wolves and baboon, for instance—provide excellently for their babies and the entire pack accepts responsibility for their welfare. The babies of grazing and browsing animals—deer, antelope, etc.

—come into the world wherever the mother happens to be feeding. The calf is born onto the grass and within a few minutes must get to its feet and travel along beside its mother. If it doesn't, it surely will die from starvation or between the teeth of a predator. Once it is able to move, its mother protects and feeds it for several months.

Most rodents and predatory mammals give birth to their babies in burrows, dens, caves or similar shelters. Many dig their own. A wolf, for instance, is quite capable of digging a burrow more than twenty feet long, well under the surface of the earth. Other animals must find a ready-made place; Felis the cougar was one of these.

Being a cat, she was not a digger, so her babies would be born in natural shelter; and this is what she sought during the early weeks of March as she traveled the length of the canyon.

The place must be just right. The first requirement was that it provide shelter from the weather. The next was that it be secluded. Although man was Felis' only enemy in the wilderness, her babies would be vulnerable to predation from many animals while she was away hunting.

If Felis had lived in other parts of the cougar's enormous range, in the dry juniper forests of the Southwest, for instance, she might have chosen a thicket of brush or tangle of tree roots as her lair. But since her home was in the canyon with its wealth of boulders, she sought a cairn—a den of rocks. She scouted several but none seemed to satisfy her. This one was too small; this, too exposed to the weather. This was too close to the canyon's humans; this, too far from her beaten trails. Then she remembered the empty rats' nest.

It was just right. The back part, under the boulders, was dry and protected from the weather. The litter which the rats had brought in during their stay would provide a warm, soft bed for the cubs. The new lair was secluded and could be easily defended, since its only access was through the narrow cleft in the rocks. It was well removed from the humans, although now, in mid-March before the trees leafed out, their cabin could be seen across the canyon and downstream. Later, it would be screened from sight by the trees.

Felis moved in one afternoon when the temperature was five degrees below zero. She was beginning to feel the pains which signaled the birth of her cubs.

Late in the night a mass of clouds drifted out of the south, carried on a warm breeze. The mountain people called the breeze a chinook. In less than an hour, the temperature rose almost forty degrees, well above freezing. Droplets of water fell from the tree branches. Snow which had lain heavily on the pines and fir all winter began to melt and slough to the ground. *PLOP. PLOP.* The branches, freed of their loads, eased back into their normal shape, slowly as though they were tired old men carefully straightening their backs. At the beaver lodge, little pools of water formed on the ice, then flowed toward the dam. The water wormed its way through the mass of twigs and mud, seeped down the dam's face, and wound around boulders on the stream bed below. It flowed as a second stream on the ice which still sheathed the main stream. It melted the snow which lay on the ice, thus adding still more water. Far downstream, at the canyon's mouth, it spread out across the meadow where the deer had wintered, forming a shallow pond on top of the snow. Later in the night, a warm rain began to fall, further melting the snow pack and feeding the stream.

The date was March 20. Every place on earth the days and nights were of equal length—twelve hours

each—as the sun crossed the equator on its north-
ward journey. It was the day of the vernal equinox.
The last of winter; the first of spring.

The warm breeze that drifted up the canyon
seemed a breath of new life after the frozen death of
winter. It hinted of crocuses and daffodils, of buds
opening into fresh, green leaves, and of babies.

In her den high on the canyon's western slope,
Felis the cougar felt the warm breeze as she lay in
labor. Just before dawn in that first night of spring,
her litter of cubs was born.

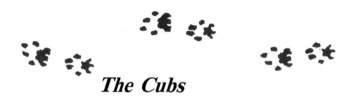

The Cubs

There were four of them, little balls of fur, each about twelve inches long and weighing one pound. Three females and one male. Four brand-new cougar cubs. Their mother, Felis, was washing them. Her big tongue slopped back and forth, up and down, across and over them, licking away the membrane in which they were encased and clearing their nostrils so they could breathe. On and on until it seemed she would scrub off their hides. The kittens objected, whining in tiny, high-pitched voices. But the sandpaper-rough tongue kept pummeling, rolling them over and pushing them away when they tried to nurse. Finally they were slick and shiny, spotlessly clean. But still she held them off and turned her attention to the placenta, the spongy tissue which had nourished the cubs while they were developing inside her and which had been expelled immediately after their birth. Felis ate it. This was part of her job as a wilderness mother. Only when the last shred of the afterbirth, as the placenta is called, was disposed of, did she flop on her side and let the cubs get to her.

They whined and fumbled blindly along her body to find the nipples. The male, who was slightly larger and stronger than his sisters, was the first to begin feeding. Ultimately, all four were lined up along her flank, tiny legs sprawled at all angles, eyes tightly sealed, sucking as hard as they could. Felis washed her face with one of her huge paws, then lay back purring, a deep, contented sound which filled the little den perched high on the canyon's slope.

She had managed the birth by herself. There was no other female cougar standing by to help and the cubs' father was miles away in his own territory, his brief honeymoon with Felis long forgotten. Even had he showed up when the cubs were born she would have driven him off.

How did the cougar know what to do? She was a very young adult, only slightly more than two years old, and this was her first litter. She had never seen other cubs being born. Yet she took care of everything from start to finish just as though she had done it all before.

Nobody can say how she knew what she needed to know. The best answer is that she operated from instinct, that knowledge which we define as natural and unreasoning. For instance, we say that a kitten is acting instinctively when it plays with a ball of yarn, or that our pet canary is singing instinctively. Until we know much more about animal behavior than we do now, this answer will have to do.

But we must not pass lightly over the word "instinct." It deserves great respect. Instinct is a source of wisdom as old as life itself. It has been passed from parent to baby for millions of years, ready when needed by the new generations to teach them to survive, individually and as a species. It teaches predators how to kill, thus we see a house kitten practicing on a ball of yarn the craft it will later turn against a mouse. It teaches birds to announce their territories by singing, so the canary, even when caged in a house, trills out a warning to other canaries. Instinct is a vital part of the magnificent process we call nature.

It taught Felis the cougar how to bring her four cubs into the world, and, in turn, directed them to her nipples.

The instinct which led them to feed was only one of many on which they would call for the rest of their lives if they were to survive. From the moment of birth the cubs were on their own. Never again would they know the complete safety they had experienced during those three months they spent inside their mother's body. True, for the first months of their lives she would feed and protect them, but they were now individual cougars and with each passing week would become more responsible for themselves.

Sixty million years of evolution had prepared them well for the task. Even at birth, all the tools they would need either already existed in their tiny bodies or were there as patterns, waiting for time and growth to unlock them—muscles, bones, claws, fangs, and in the very heart of their being, the wilderness wisdom they would call on for the hunt.

The cubs were dark brown, with rows of darker, almost black, spots on their bodies and equally dark rings around their tails. In time, the brown coats would lighten to fawn-color, and the markings fade and, at about one year, would almost disappear, although some fully grown cougars still carry faint indications of them. Scientists think that these spots and rings are remnants of some striped ancestor of the cougar who wore them as camouflage—protective coloration. Perhaps in those days the habitat was such as to encourage a striped pattern, much as the tiger's is today. But cougars are animals which live with deer now, and they have evolved an unmarked body coloring that is almost identical with that of their prey.

During the first few weeks of their lives, the cubs did little except nurse, sleep and try to stay warm.

Mostly, they slept. Several times a day they would
nuzzle their mother's body, nurse, then fall asleep,
often while still fastened onto the nipples. If she were
away hunting, they slept in a ball, entwined for
warmth. When she returned, and they sensed her
body, they would mew pitiously and push each other
aside in their haste to eat. As they lay nursing at her
side, they kneaded her flanks with their front feet,
first one then the other, just as house kittens do. Then
the sweet milk would come down and they would fill
their tiny stomachs.

The world they lived in was a black void with only
the feel, scent and taste of their mother for company,
for they had been born with their eyes closed. About
eight days later, the eyes began to open. Not all at
once, of course, At first, just the merest hint of light
slipped past their eyelids, and the black world faded
to gray. There were no shapes as yet in this world,
just light. Gradually, the eyelids opened farther and
the light grew. At two weeks, their eyes were completely open and they could see each other and their
mother as indistinct black shapes against the light.
They still couldn't focus and their eyes were milky
blue, not the living, translucent green they would
become one day. But the darkness was gone.

Light was also returning to the world outside the
den, as the sun climbed higher in the sky and stayed
up longer with each passing day. Winter was dying.

The chinook that had drifted out of the south on
the night of the cubs' birth lasted only until the following afternoon, when the temperature suddenly
dropped far below freezing. The water formed from
the melting snow froze hard, creating a condition
called "silver thaw" by the mountain people. Each
willow stem and branchlet which had glistened
wetly during the chinook was encased in a sheath of
ice. The surface of the beaver pond became a glassy-

smooth mirror. Along the lower reaches of the stream where the melted water had spread out, a glazing of new ice gleamed in the sun which rose the following morning. The canyon glistened and sparkled in its dressing of ice—a world of cold, frozen beauty.

But to the wild animals it was one of the most dangerous of all of nature's harsh conditions. The seeds and grass were locked beneath a coating of ice which the rodents and deer could not break through. So they went hungry. A yearling deer wandered onto the glazing of ice downstream. She fell and broke a leg. Two coyotes found her and were joined by four glistening ravens which continually swept the canyon's length looking for whatever the predators left. The boy of the human family found the yearling's remains as he trudged home from school. And that night, Felis the cougar drove away an ermine which had come to feed on the carcass, then finished it. Although she normally killed her own meat, she would also eat carrion if it were not tainted. Finally, a wolverine, waddling through the forest, hungry as all the canyon's creatures were, stripped the carcass of flesh and even gnawed on the bones, taking the last vestiges of nourishment from the marrow. So the yearling, through her tragic accident brought on by the silver thaw, provided food for eight other animals.

On the third day after the heavy freeze, the weather warmed again and the sound of melting snow filled the canyon. *Drip, drop.* From countless fir branches, willow twigs and stems of last year's grass the water fell to the snow pack, softening and dissolving it. The layer of ice locking off the stream began to rot and patches of open water appeared. A pond formed at the canyon's mouth where the influx of water became dammed behind a log that had

At one month the cougar kitten has the baby hair, spots and ringed tail of infancy.

Wilford Miller

Ernest Wilkinson

Cougars, as many wild animals, are caring, strict mothers. The misbehaving baby can expect to be cuffed or picked up by the nape and forced to behave.

fallen across the stream during the previous autumn. The log lay in shade, shielded from the sun, and the ice and snow were frozen solidly around it. The pond grew, flooding the deer's feeding area and forcing them back up onto the slopes. Then it topped the crude ice dam, spilled over and during one day, wore it down. The pond disappeared.

Bare patches of earth appeared on the canyon's southern slopes. The black earth steamed in the spring sun and little creatures—mice and voles, snow buntings and rabbits—came to eat the seeds left over from last summer. The red-tailed hawks swept up the canyon from their wintering grounds in the valley to the east. They saw the animals feeding in the bare patches of earth. They folded their wings and dived to the attack.

By mid-April, when the cougar cubs were one month old, all of the canyon which was exposed to the sun lay bare, although snow was still piled deep among the trees and along shaded twistings of the stream. But the game trails which wound down the hillsides were clear and the southern faces of the boulders lay warm and inviting in the sun.

The cubs had grown tremendously in their four weeks of life. They weighed about five pounds each and were fat little balls of spotted fur. They spent each day outside the den, playing on the ledge with bits of cottonwood fluff which the den's previous tenants—the rats—had carried home. They batted them back and forth with their paws, running and jumping, clumsy, awkward. They fought mock battles with each other, biting and clawing with baby teeth and the still soft claws. Now and then one bit or swiped a little too hard. There would be a squeal of pain, an angry snarl, and a serious battle would break out. More often than not it was broken up by Felis, who was lying on the ledge, watching over the babies. She would rise, open her enormous mouth and grab one of the guilty parties by the nape of the neck. The cub would hang there, paws draped in front of its chest, to be carried back into the den.

But Felis still had to hunt, now more than usual since she had not only herself to feed, but four hungry cubs as well. So she wasn't always at home. It was on one such occasion that the bear found her family.

The black bear lived farther upstream in the canyon where she had slept away the winter in a cave. Sometime during her sleep, she had given birth to two cubs, tiny, naked creatures who looked more like pigs than the bears they would grow into. The cubs had to fend for themselves for several weeks, nursing and staying warm at their sleeping mother's body. Finally, in April, she awoke, thin and ravenous from her many weeks' fast. Her first response to the world outside her den was to eat. Just about anything. The bear, as many creatures in the world, including man, was omniverous, that is, her diet included almost anything edible—fish, red meat, berries, birds' eggs, whatever.

The bear came from her den one morning, followed by her two cubs. In the weeks since their birth, the twins had grown thick coats of black fur and had fattened. Side by side, they trailed after their mother as she wandered down the side of the hill to the stream. She searched the banks for dead fish or other carcasses. But the melting snow had swept the stream clean. She prowled the quiet backwaters for frogs, but it was much too early in the season. Still, her hunger had to be satisfied. Then she remembered the nest of wood rats she had raided the previous summer. She crossed the stream and trotted into the forest. The cubs hesitated on the far side of the stream. What to their mother was a shallow crossing represented a major barrier to them. They whined.

The female stopped and looked back. *Wuff!* she commanded. First one cub, then the other plopped into the ice cold water and half-swam, half-waded across.

The bear led them uphill toward the pile of boulders that housed the rats' nest. She remembered that she had had to squeeze through a narrow cleft in the rocks, then cross a ledge to reach the nest. After two false turns, she recognized the opening between two boulders. She turned to the cubs. *Wuff!* "Wait here." They found a convenient tree and shinnied to the upper branches. Their mother walked through the passageway. It was easy, thin as she was from her winter's fast.

At the far end of the cleft, she emerged into the sunlight, turned sharply to her right, and began crossing the narrow ledge which led to the nest. Something had changed since her visit to the place nine months earlier. There were no rats scurrying away at her approach, no frantic squealing, no odor of rat droppings. The bear stopped to study the situation. The rats were gone. But something was living here. She peered into the den at the end of the ledge, trying to pierce its dim interior with her nearsighted eyes. She saw movement, little fluffs of brown fur that seemed to be playing together. She moved closer. Then she recognized the objects as four one-month-old cougar cubs.

The bear had raided a cougar den once before, in this same canyon, and had killed and eaten two cubs. They were orphans, mewing for their dead mother who, even then, was stretched out in the back of a wagon driven by a little man with a broken nose, a bounty hunter who had treed her with his dogs, then finished her with a rifle. That had happened two years earlier and since then, there had been no cougar in the canyon. Now there were four undefended cubs. Although an adult cougar could give the bear a hard fight, the young, as the young of just about any animal, were very much a part of her diet if she could find them when the mother was away.

She grunted and moved across the ledge, her eyes fixed on the cubs. At the sound, they whirled around, expecting to see their mother, but saw instead a huge, black mass moving in on them. They leaped back against the den's far wall, and at the same instant, yelped a shrill whistle-like call, a sound which cougar cubs make when startled. They crouched against each other in terror. The little male curved his lips back in a babyish snarl and hissed at the bear. She continued to inch across the ledge. She reached the den's entrance and swiped with one paw to scoop up a cub. They were out of reach, far back in the den. She swiped again, then scrunched down and shoved her snout into the den. The cubs flattened themselves against the rock and the little male hissed his defiance. The bear pushed herself farther into the den. A snap of her teeth missed the smallest of the cubs by a fraction of an inch. She shoved herself closer with her hind feet and prepared to grab again.

Suddenly her back and rump exploded in searing pain. A pair of teeth clamped down on her neck. The bear grunted and tried to back out of the den. Again and again her backside was raked. She grunted again and, with a final effort, tore her head free of the entrance. She tried to wheel around to face whatever was attacking her, but the ledge outside the den was too narrow. She reared onto her hind legs and, in standing, swung against the boulder's face. She felt a final, excruciating pain rake across her back and then she was free. She turned to see Felis crouched on the ledge, braced to leap at her again.

The cougar had been running down a rabbit along the stream when she heard the shrill whistle of alarm from her cubs. She wheeled and raced up the hillside. Powerful, fifteen-foot-long bounds swept her up through the trees and into the sunlight at the foot of the boulder where the den was hidden. She could have run around the rock and through the cleft, but that would have taken too much time. Without slowing, she leaped twenty feet up the face of the boulder and scrambled onto the ledge. There in front of her was the bear's huge black rump, sticking out from the den. Felis jumped and fastened herself, fang and claw, onto the hairy hide. She raked with her back feet, tearing fur and skin apart. When the bear finally stood, she was knocked onto the ledge where she crouched to face the invader.

This was no cool, passionless hunt for food. This was the life-and-death issue of her cubs' safety. Felis bared her teeth and lowered her ears. Anger at the massive black hulk looming over her burned in her eyes. She raised a paw and swiped viciously at the air. She hissed.

The bear was frantic from her pain and the danger she recognized in the furious cougar. She dropped to all four feet and lunged at Felis. The cougar raked her snout, then backed away. The bear lunged again, and again was raked. Blood poured from her wounded muzzle and her back. All she wanted to do was escape, but the way was blocked by the enraged cat. The bear looked at the wall behind her. Straight up. She looked the other way. Twenty feet, almost straight down. But she had to get away from those slashing claws. She eased herself over the edge, was slashed again on the flank by the cougar, then, half-sliding, half-falling, tumbled to the ground, leaving a trail of blood smeared along the face of the rock.

She lay still for several minutes, stunned by the fall. At last, she stood and waddled painfully downhill. At the stream, she plunged in to bathe her wounds. Later, she circled far around the den site to the tree where her cubs waited. *Wuff!* She called them down and led them far upstream. Her wounds would heal, but never again did she venture near the rats' nest in the boulders.

When the bear slid from the ledge, Felis watched until it rose and disappeared down the hill. She sniffed the tufts of coarse black hair she had torn from the bear's back. Then she turned to her cubs, still huddled against the den's back wall. She licked each of them, over and over, washed their backs and faces, tumbled them onto their bellies, licked some more. At the touch of the familiar tongue, their terror faded and hunger took over. The little male hissed and tried to fight the tongue, wanting a nipple instead. Felis bowled him over with one cuff of her paw, its terrible claws now sheathed. She pinned him to the den floor and washed him again, stem to stern. Then she lay back and let the four babies nurse. The fire died from her eyes, and as the cubs kneaded her belly and drew on her nipples, she began to purr with contentment. The battle was over and won. The cubs were safe. Life went on.

During the last week of April, spring came suddenly and dramatically to the canyon. New grass sprouted on the southern slopes. Catkins, called pussywillows, formed on the willows. Buds appeared on bare trees and bushes, then suddenly, as though overnight, burst their shells. Seen from a distance the aspen seemed veiled in fine, green gossamer as their new, lime-green leaves fanned out in the warm sunshine. Lichens, clinging to the boulders, changed from drab brown to summer reds, oranges, yellows and greens. The lichen was actually two plants: a fungus which contains the acid that breaks down rocks into soil, and an alga which manufactures food. Together, these two formed a symbiotic relationship in which each member contributed to the welfare of the whole. There are many such relationships in the animal and plant worlds.

Along the still backwaters of the stream, spring was announced each evening by the croakings of bull-frogs. They filled their air sacs and in loud burps brought the night alive. *Garump! Garump!* Already, masses of their jelly were floating in the pools, each containing hundreds of eggs. Mosquito larvae floated below the surface of the water and tiny minnows darted among them, gulping down thousands. But other thousands lived on to become the pesky insects which would plague the canyon's animals, human and non-human, throughout the summer. The year's crop of babies made their appearance. Puff-tailed rabbits, each no larger than a child's hand. Muskrats, bare-tailed and beady-eyed. Wood rats, mice, squir-rels and chipmunks, all naked and helpless, and still confined to their burrows. Prairie dog babies popped their heads out of the holes in the colony tunneled into the sandy hillside at the mouth of the canyon.

Summer's birds began to appear, winging up the canyon singly and in small groups, to set up territo-ries and warble, chirp or caw their songs of warning to others of their kind. Red-tailed hawks and golden eagles took up their predation. Sparrows replaced the juncos. Red-winged blackbirds clung to the new reeds growing along the edges of the beaver pond and in the marsh at the canyon's mouth. Western bluebirds darted from the aspen, harvesting last year's dry grass to build nests for the eggs forming inside the females' bodies. Robins probed the moist bottomlands for earthworms and trilled to each pass-ing rain shower.

And the deer drifted back to their summer ranges. They wandered up in small groups, nibbling the grass as they came and trailed by spindly-legged fawns. The bucks had already gone to the high coun-

San Diego Zoo

Cougar kittens develop rapidly. This
two-month-old baby already is losing the soft,
downy hair of infancy, although the dark
spots will take many months to fade and
disappear.

try where they would wander until next autumn's
rutting season brought them down to collect harems.
They had shed their antlers and at first glance were
indistinguishable from the does except for the tiny
buds of the new antlers on their heads.

Springtime filled the canyon, warm and green,
alive with the chirping, trilling, buzzing, nibbling of
a thousand different species—birds, insects, fish,
mammals—all bursting with life.

For Felis the cougar, the newly born season meant
nothing but more work, for her cubs were weaned
now and needed meat; yet they were a long, long
way from being able to hunt for themselves. Felis
had started the weaning process four weeks earlier
when the cubs were one month old, and it proved to
be most difficult. The cubs were used to her rich,
warm milk and so far as they were concerned, this
was the only thing which qualified as food. But she
persisted and by early May they were squabbling
among themselves for red meat she killed and led
them to. The cubs weighed ten pounds each now.
Their feet seemed too big for their bodies and they
stumbled all over themselves as they rough-housed
inside the den or on the ledge outside. In fact, the
den itself was becoming overcrowded. It was one
thing for the adult cougar to live there with four little
balls of fur. But after those balls became overgrown,
clumsy youngsters rapidly approaching adolescence,
the situation was quite different. One afternoon
when she was going out to hunt she called the cubs
to her. One by one they left the den and crossed the
narrow ledge which had so nicely protected them
from the outside world, but which also had barred
them from it. The male was the first cub across, step-
ping out in rather a cocky manner, as though he had
crossed narrow ledges every day of his young life. His
three sisters were much more timid and worked
their way across the ledge, crowding against the wall

until they were safely through the cleft in the rocks. At the upper end of the cleft they found their mother waiting, and when she moved down the side of the hill, they trailed along behind her. They didn't know it at the time, but that was the last they would see of the den. From that moment on they would truly be wilderness babies.

Felis led them down to the stream, where she crouched to drink. The cubs hadn't seen flowing water before. Curious as all babies, especially cougar babies, they had to investigate. The male swiped at the stream with a paw, then jumped back as he flipped water on his face. He tumbled head over heels into the grass. He got up and tried it again. The inevitable happened. *SPLASH!* He tumbled in. Felis walked into the stream and grabbed him by the scruff of the neck. She carried him to the far bank and dumped him on the sand where he sat, wet and bedraggled, looking very unhappy. Felis called the other cubs across. But they held back, and paced along the far bank. Finally, one gave a tremendous leap, almost cleared the stream, kerplunked into the water and was dragged out by her mother. The other two cubs simply would not cross, so Felis had to wade across and carry them.

On the far bank, she groomed the two wet cubs until they were fluffy dry. Then she moved slowly along the bushes beside the stream, hoping to raise a rabbit or porcupine. A snowshoe rabbit broke cover. Its white winter coat had changed to the dull grays and browns of summer and only by carefully watching and racing close behind was Felis able to see it as it twisted up the hill. The rabbit zigged sharply to the left. Felis cut across to intercept it. The rabbit zagged right. Felis spun in her tracks and closed in. A final, miscalculated turn by the rabbit and Felis had him. She called the cubs to her kill and they came running awkwardly up from the stream.

The little male claimed the rabbit as his own, but the females objected, and a tug-of-war was on. The male growled and tried to pull away the prize. The three females overwhelmed him and he was slowly, unwillingly, dragged down the hill. In the end they compromised and each ripped and chewed at the carcass as Felis stood by. When their bellies were filled and they had finally quit playing with the rabbit, she led them farther up the slope toward the summer range of the deer. That afternoon she killed a doe near the boulder overlooking Burned Clearing and she and the cubs fed from it for almost a week.

The boulder became home base just as it had the previous summer, but since Felis was a wandering animal she and her family often were away for several days at a time. In the beginning, she set an easy pace for the cubs, just a few miles a day. They were still small and everything in the forest was new and exciting to them. They investigated blades of grass and the smallest crevice in each boulder. They nosed fir cones, dry and empty from the previous year, and the melting patches of snow tucked in shaded corners of the canyon. The jumble of fallen trees in Burned Clearing was especially intriguing, enormous toys in a gigantic, fifty-acre playground. The cubs climbed over and around them, explored the thousand tunnels created when the trees had fallen, jackstraw fashion, in the fire many years ago. They played tag and follow-the-leader and set up mock ambushes for each other. The male was especially aggressive in this game. He would lie in wait for his sisters to pass, then as they drew near, would squirm his tiny rump, get set, and leap out at them. Biting, pawing, growling, rolling downhill locked together until a leaf blew past or a bit of bark fell from a log. Then the fighters separated to investigate this new thing which had invaded their world.

It was in Burned Clearing that the male first learned about porcupines. The hard way.

One day while he was chasing his sisters, the cub saw a quilled tail sticking from beneath a log. He forgot the game of tag and walked around the log, head angled to one side, curious and cocky. There, on the other side of the log, stood a porcupine, propped on his hind legs, methodically stripping bark from an aspen, looking neither right nor left, totally absorbed in the task at hand. The cub had never seen such a creature. Slowly and very cautiously he approached. When he was two feet away, the porcupine looked down, saw that he had company and dropped into his defensive posture—rump faced toward the cub, quills extended, tail flailing. The cub cocked his head, first to one side, then the other. Here, it seemed, was a new playmate. He reached forward with a paw. The porcupine's tail made contact. *YEOW!* The cub leaped back with three quills in his paw. He turned tail and ran toward the boulder where his mother had been sleeping. At his whistle-like scream, she snapped awake and bounded into the clearing. She met the cub as he was half-running, half-limping out from among the fallen trees. He was whining with pain. Felis licked his face and head, but that was not where the trouble was. Back on the boulder, he licked his paw and quite inadvertently, pulled one of the quills with his baby teeth. Another had been dislodged as he crossed the rough boulder. The third broke off with its barbed shaft imbedded in one of the cub's toes. A few days later the wound festered and the cub could barely walk. But he was a very healthy baby and eventually the broken quill worked its way through the skin and out the top of his toe. The cub healed perfectly, but he never played with a porcupine again.

By the end of May, when the cubs were ten weeks

old, Felis was taking them far afield from Burned
Clearing. One day she picked up the trail of the boy
on his way to school. The cubs followed along as she
moved up the narrow, dirt road in the wake of the
strange odor. It was very new to the cubs, this smell
of a human, and at first they were nervous. But, seeing that their mother didn't mind it, they soon lost
interest and straggled behind. They nosed the new
vegetation springing up alongside the road; they
stumbled awkwardly after a rabbit which scampered
from the bushes; they watched the ravens who
scolded them from high atop the fir trees.

Felis cut away from the boy's trail at her usual
place and climbed the hill above the little ranch. The
last time she had visited the spot was in deep winter,
well before the cubs were born. Her favorite rock
had been covered with snow and the valley beyond
was frozen into a black and white stillness like an
etching created by an old Dutch artist—the black-
ness of the fir and naked trees standing stark and
rigid in the whiteness of the snow-buried world.

Now it was different. The valley was alive with
muted sound. The far-off laughing of children playing near the school. The squeaking of a wheel as the
rancher drove away in his wagon. The sound of men
working on the railroad. And there was color. The
precise, dark green of the firs, formal as soldiers on
review. Brilliant bursts of yellow and orange of the
flowers blooming along the fence lines. The smoky,
pale blue of sagebrush that crowded a little road
where it topped the hill to the east. The crisp, lime
green of aspen and cottonwood leaves, and over all,
a cloudless, intensely blue sky.

The four cougar cubs found a pile of last year's
leaves that the wind had whipped into the lee of a
boulder. It became their playground. They ran and
jumped over, through, under it, chasing each other.

Felis chose a less strenuous activity. She leaped lightly onto her favorite boulder and sprawled in the sunshine, studying the ranch below and the little valley beyond it. Not that she could appreciate the springtime colors splashed across the mountains. As many animals, Felis was color-blind, or at least scientists assumed that she was. Her world was made of gradations of gray, from the charcoal, almost black, grays of the forest's dense shadows, to the pale, almost white gray of the sky. But, never having known color, she didn't miss it. And, despite her color-blindness, her vision was extremely keen. She was as much at home during the darkest night as in sunlight and she could catch the slightest flicker of movement in her world. Her hearing was superb also, and as she perfected her woodcraft, she learned to distinguish one sound from another. If she were hunting, the flutter of a bird's wing was passed over and ignored. But the crack of a twig made by a deer's hoof would make her freeze on the spot until she learned the source of the sound. And, of course, as a predator living in the wilderness, her sense of smell was excellent. Sight, hearing, smell, all her senses were honed to perfection.

Blessed as she was, she should have been aware of the boy long before he reached the top of her hill that afternoon. But she was sleeping. The cubs had long since given up their romping and were off in the forest curled up asleep. The day was filled with the lazy droning of insects and the warm sunshine. Felis' belly was filled with the deer meat she had eaten late the night before. Everything combined to make the day ideal for a deep sleep.

While she slept, the boy left school and started the long walk home to his cabin. At the game trail where Felis always turned away from the road, he hesitated, then followed the trail through the forest. He

climbed the hill overlooking the the village. At the
top, he crawled onto a rock and lay on his stomach,
watching the activity far below in the village. He,
too, fell asleep in the sunshine. Later he awoke and
saw the cougar, and as he moved to get a better look
at her, he dislodged a small stone.

Felis jerked awake. She snapped her head around
and saw the boy less than fifty feet away, looking
directly at her. She had seen him many times as she
followed his trail, but he had always been unaware of
her. And she had never been so close to him. Now she
lay staring at him. The seconds passed. Half a minute.
Felis felt none of the panic she had known many
months earlier when the hunters almost killed her.
Neither was there any of the nervous rage which had
run through her when she sniffed their dead dog. But
still, this was a human lying on the rock just fifty feet
away and despite the many weeks Felis had trailed
him on his way to school, she felt uneasy in his pres-
ence. The longer she lay there, the greater her dis-
comfort became. Finally, she stood and leaped from
the rock. She reached the forest in three bounds and
the boy was hidden by the screen of trees. Felis
called to her cubs in a low growl which meant, "No
nonsense now. Come here!" They tumbled from
their sleep and came running. She led them back to
Burned Clearing along a game trail which swung far
to one side of the road which the boy would walk. She
had had enough of him for one day.

When summer came to the canyon she realized
that he was following her. One morning in July she
found his footprints in the soft earth beside one of her
scrapes. Another time, she smelled him on the trunk
of her favorite scratching tree. Later, he apparently
found one of her kills, for when she returned to eat
from it, the dirt and twigs had been removed, then
clumsily put back in place. But, despite his efforts to

find her, the boy didn't get close, for Felis never again allowed herself to be caught napping as she had that afternoon in spring.

July. Summer lay hot on the canyon. Daytime temperatures climbed into the eighties and low nineties, then slipped twenty degrees and more at night. Dust gathered on the leaves and grass, turning their deep, rich greenery to the color of weathered copper—a hazy, soft green. Pine and fir trees filled the air with the tangy odor of the forest. Aspen and cottonwood leaves drooped in the heat. Summer's flowers bloomed for a week or two, then faded. Bluebells, wild roses, chokecherries, sage. The low-growing bitterroot which was the state's official flower, opened its cactus-like, rosy blossoms high on the exposed southern slopes of the canyon. Many years earlier, the Indians had harvested the plant's starchy tap roots for food. Now, bears occasionally grubbed them from the earth.

The riotous growth of springtime had passed, leaving the canyon and its inhabitants—plant and animal —a few weeks of summer in which to mature and ripen for winter. Seeds formed in the grasses and annual flowering plants. Cones grew fat on coniferous trees. Berries and nuts swelled with nourishment from the parent plants. And among the animals, the springtime's crop of babies was growing toward adulthood. In the smaller species, such as the mice, chipmunks, rats and ground squirrels, the babies were already adults, ready to breed. A hundred different species of young birds were testing and strengthening their wings. The smaller ones—sparrows, robins, bluebirds—were already proficient, darting back and forth from tree to ground, catching insects in mid-air, probing in the earth or scratching seeds according to the feeding habits of their kind.

The larger birds—hawks, eagles, owls—still had to

care for their young and would for several weeks. Some of these chicks were making awkward, half-hearted attempts to fly, but they had many weeks of trial and failure ahead before they could hunt for themselves.

Among the larger mammals—the bears and cougar, coyote and lynxes, deer and elk—the babies, although weaned and able to follow their mothers, still could not fend for themselves. The young deer and elk would be self-sufficient by winter. Bear and cougar cubs would have still one more year with their mothers.

During the hot summer days, the prey animals became more active in the early morning and late afternoon. During the day they holed up to keep cool. Burrowing creatures stayed below ground; deer and elk retired to the thick bushes and trees to escape the heat. So the predators matched their prey's timing. Coyotes, Felis the cougar, the hawks and eagles—all those who lived by killing other animals—were out very early in the morning and again late in the evening. In midday, they too slept.

One afternoon an electrical storm swept up the canyon. Huge cumulus clouds formed on the southern skyline, built and climbed fifteen thousand feet into the clear, hot sky, then marched forward as a conquering, airborne army. The air began to stir, jostling the drooping leaves, sighing among the pines and fir. The temperature dropped and the hot, dusty odors of summer gave way to the cool anticipation of rain. The wind rose, ruffling tiny pools of water into miniature whitecapped seas, and bending the grasses and reeds. The droning of a million insects died away; the birds quieted. There was a momentary hush. Then the storm hit. Lightning bolts streaked from the clouds, followed by the ear-shattering explosion of thunder. A tree was split open, top to bottom. The wind rose, bringing with it sheets of warm, heavy rain. Dust devils swirled into life and walked daintily up the canyon's trail. Then the pounding rain beat them into the ground. A fir tree, standing in the beaver pond was toppled, pinning and killing one of the beaver's pups. The tree itself had been destroyed years before when the beaver's pond drowned its roots.

The canyon's small birds huddled in the shelter of tree branches, their heads tucked under wings, feathers fluffed out. A golden eagle mother remained stoically in her nest at the top of an exposed boulder, wings half spread to protect her two chicks. Deer and elk, cougar and badger, all sought shelter. Only the old beaver kept on about his business, felling trees, then towing them back to the damaged dam, unaware of the tragedy that had struck his family.

The storm lasted for an hour, then passed. The wind died; the rain stopped as suddenly as it had begun; the thunder faded. Sunlight peeked from behind the thick, scudding clouds. The canyon lay damp and clean, spread out to dry in the warm, sweet air. Droplets of water fell from leaves and grass. Steam rose from wet, hot boulders.

Gradually, bird song and insect droning rose as the canyon's creatures spread their wings, ruffled feathers, fluffed fur and shook themselves dry. A robin swooped down to the wet bottomlands where earthworms were inching up out of their drowned tunnels. The robin stood, head cocked to catch a hint of movement or the tiny sound of a burrowing worm, then darted forward, probed the earth with its beak and drew out a wet, wiggling worm. A rabbit ventured from the bushes and nibbled at the fresh, wet grass. High on the canyon's slopes, the golden eagle lifted from her nest and glided down the canyon. She spotted the rabbit, swooped down and caught it in

The wolverine *(Gulo gulo)*, although much
smaller than bears and cougar, has been
known to drive them away from their kills.

her talons, then winged heavily back to the nest to feed her ever-hungry brood. She dropped the rabbit in the nest, then flew away on another hunt. The chicks tore at the carcass, and one of them, in his ravenous frenzy, pushed it over the edge of the nest. It hung there for a moment, then tumbled down the face of the boulder, hit the sloping ground at the base and rolled downhill until it lodged against a tree trunk. The eaglets screamed their frustration, but since they were unable to fly, they had to wait for their mother to bring more food.

Felis the cougar and her four cubs found the rabbit a few minutes later as they were walking along the slope. The male cub dashed forward and started to tear at it and was quickly joined by his three sisters. Felis flopped in the grass to wait for the cubs. But another of the canyon's citizens had smelled the rabbit and was scurrying uphill from the stream.

He was a wolverine, one of the toughest and rarest animals in all of North America. The wolverine was a member of the weasel family. He weighed about forty pounds and measured slightly more than three feet long. He had a shaggy, dark brown coat that was banded along each side by a light, chestnut-colored streak of fur. He had a bushy tail, sharp claws, a blunt, bear-like snout, tiny, nearsighted eyes and a pair of small ears. He would eat and fight just about anything that walked, crawled or flew. To the Indians, he was a devil and they claimed that if a person looked into his eyes, that person would go mad. Trappers hated him because he killed and spoiled animals caught in the traps. Yet, even today, wolverines are important to one group of people, the Arctic Eskimos. Because wolverine fur does not ice, the Eskimos use a strip of it to line the edges of their parkas —the edges which contact their faces—to prevent their breath from freezing on their clothing.

As a member of the weasel family the wolverine is a carnivore which will either kill its own meat or eat what some other animal has hunted down. If a wolverine decides he wants someone else's prey, he usually gets it.

The wolverine which smelled the dead rabbit that Felis' cubs were eating, decided the rabbit would be his dinner. He waddled up the hill and burst through the trees, less than fifty feet from the spot where the four cougar cubs were tearing at the carcass. Still, he didn't see the cubs, for he had poor vision and depended heavily on his excellent sense of smell to hunt his food. He stopped at the forest's edge, stood on his hind legs and peered toward the rabbit, putting one paw to his eyes in order to shade them from the sun. Then he spotted the cubs. He growled and dashed toward them.

The cubs heard him coming. They looked up, saw him, and jumped aside, expecting their mother to take care of this intruder, as she had taken care of all their problems thus far. But Felis had encountered the wolverine much earlier, just a few weeks after arriving in the canyon. She knew what he was—fearless, aggressive, a formidable fighter. She wanted nothing to do with him. So the one hundred-fifty pound cougar gave way to the forty-pound wolverine, taking her cubs with her, leaving the field and the day to one of the toughest animals in North America.

By late August when the cubs were approaching their sixth month, they were gangly adolescents with enormous feet and ears. The baby spots were fading and the long, heavy tails of adulthood were beginning to develop. The male weighed about forty pounds and his sisters ranged between twenty and thirty-five.

Each cub had its own personality.

The male was the largest and most aggressive. He dashed into situations when the females held back, and took risks they chose to avoid. But his aggressive spirit was tempered by good sense. If ordered to obey by Felis, he did so immediately, as on that afternoon when she saw the boy.

One of the females was almost his equal. She was larger than her sisters and always finished at least in second place in the rough-and-tumble games, when chasing a ground squirrel, or when called to dinner. Now and then, she actually beat out her brother.

Of the other two, one was a frivolous little creature without a brain in her head, or so it seemed. A lovable, good-natured dimwit. And the fourth cub, the runt, was equally pitiful. Smaller than the others, she was always last—whether at Felis' nipples during the nursing days at the den site, or tearing apart a deer later. Always trying very hard, but never having quite enough strength or good sense.

Felis treated them alike—lovingly stern. At this stage in their development there was little time for baby games. A very serious business was beginning; the cubs were learning to hunt.

They had been playing at hunting since they were able to move around. First, it had been the "tail game" back at the den site during their early babyhood. As Felis lay sunning or sleeping, the cubs climbed all over her, and finally they discovered her long, heavy tail with its black tip. The tip was often in motion, swishing back and forth, and to the cubs, it became an object of the hunt. They pounced on it, grappled with it, hung on to it with their front paws and clawed with the rear claws. And the more they teased and pummeled the tail, the more active it became. The tail game. The beginning of a long learning experience.

Next, they chased stray leaves and bits of fluff

which twirled and danced in the breeze at the den site. Jumping up on their hind feet to grab. Losing interest as soon as the object was caught. Back at it when the wind sent it swirling away.

They hunted each other, lying in ambush, then pouncing out as they would when they were true hunters.

Over and over the games went on. Gradually, the cubs developed the motor control and coordination which were the entire point of the games. First, the eyes must see the object, judge its distance and follow it if it were moving. Then, the muscles of the legs had to move the body ahead in just the correct lunge —not too short, not too far. The eyes saw the prey and the muscles captured it. Over and over again.

When Felis took them from the den site, their world opened a thousandfold, and soon they were pouncing on insects and small rodents. The male made the four cubs' first kill—a mouse. And he kept the others away from his prize with low, warning growls. On another occasion, he almost had a half-grown rabbit cornered, and was moving in for the kill, when the rabbit came out at him, landed a thumping blow on his chest with her powerful hind legs, leaped over him and was gone.

Then, in September, they had their first serious lesson. Not that Felis decided that the time was ripe for their education. That would come later when she often would take out one cub at a time to teach it to hunt, and the lessons would go on for as long as the cubs stayed with her. The first lesson was accidental. The family came upon a porcupine when their bellies were empty, and with dinner so close at hand, Felis set out to teach. She shoved one paw under the porcupine and, with the same motion, flipped it onto its back, exposing the unprotected belly. One swipe with her claws killed the porcupine and disemboweled it. The cubs watched.

Cougar and beaver. So long as the beaver
stays in the water, it is relatively safe from
being caught.

Of course, not all the hunting lessons were so successful. As most predatory animals, Felis failed several times for each kill. The case of the stranded beaver was a case in point. One day, the cougar family visited the pond at the head of the canyon, hoping to catch a beaver away from the water. Trapped on solid earth, the beaver became awkward, an easy mark for a cougar. But in the water, it was an entirely different matter. There were no beaver far away from the pond that day when Felis and the cubs visited. But they did discover a situation which promised to ease the hunger pangs in their bellies. The beaver family was busy in the early autumn sunshine, reinforcing the dam, cutting saplings for food. Because the area near the dam site was already logged off, the beavers were working far upstream, almost at the end of the pond. The big male was in an especially dangerous place—a tiny inlet off to one side of the main pond. He was felling an aspen, which he planned to float the length of the pond and push into a weakened spot in the dam. He saw Felis and the cubs walking along the bank toward him, and being a wise beaver, he left the tree and plopped into the water, which was much too shallow at that point for his liking, but far better than becoming trapped on dry land. Felis bounded ahead of her family and leaped into the water after him. The cubs lined up along the shore to watch mother make a kill. It didn't prove quite that simple.

The cougar leaped toward the beaver, head held high, watching the prey. When she was within striking range, she jumped clear of the water, then came down with all four feet, trying to pin him. But the beaver slipped away and moved toward deeper water and freedom. Felis trapped him under an overhanging bank and reached in to hook him out with a paw. The beaver nipped her with his razor-sharp incisor teeth. These teeth, common to all rodents,

were the beaver's tree-cutting tools, kept razor sharp
by being honed against each other—top and bottom.
They would continue growing during his entire life.

Felis leaped back from the bite and the beaver
swam past her. She splashed after him for a few feet,
then felt the bottom sliding away beneath her as the
beaver reached deep water. Disgusted, the cougar
gave up the chase and half-walked, half-swam to the
bank where her cubs were waiting. The failure was
all in a day's business, and there might be another
time when the beaver did not fare quite so well.

Later that day, the cougars found one of the black
bear's cubs freshly dead at the foot of a tree from
which it had fallen. So instead of beaver, they ate
bear meat that night.

Now and then, between hunting lessons, she took
the cubs to the boulder overlooking the village. She
seemed to enjoy lying on the rock to watch the little
valley and the ranch at its near end. The two horses
grazing in the pasture kept her interested by the
hour. Cougars have been known to kill horses, and
ranchers claim that once a cougar acquires a taste for
horseflesh, it will continue killing them for as long as
it lives. But in most cases, the killers of livestock are
old cougars, those whose teeth are worn back to the
point where the cats can no longer hunt.

On one of Felis' visits she was seen by the dogs
which the rancher kept for his bounty hunting. They
began barking, which brought their owner from the
house just in time to see the cougar disappear behind
a rock. The bounty hunter went back into the house
and made his plans.

September. The dry, hot days which the mountain
people call dog days. No rain; little relief from the
heat. Even in the mountains time seemed to stand
still in the long, drowsy afternoons. But this stillness
was in appearance only. For the canyon's creatures
were preparing for winter. Among the insects, the

Wilford Miller

A six-month-old cougar kitten sharpens its claws on a log. The spots of babyhood are still very evident.

year's business was almost finished. Eggs were laid and the adults stayed on for a few days or weeks, droning back and forth in the sunshine. Bees gathered the very last nectar and carried it to the hives hidden in hollow trees and secluded clefts among the rocks. Grasshoppers bored tiny holes in the earth and deposited hundreds of eggs in each hole, then hopped away to die. Crawlers, swimmers, fliers, skippers, all had responded to the light and heat of summer; they had mated, fulfilled their egg-laying roles and now at the end of summer, were passing from the scene.

The small, flowering plants were done for the year. They had grown rapidly in the warmth and wetness of spring, had blossomed in summer and seduced the insects which would pollinate them. They had developed their seeds and broadcast them onto the soil. Now they stood, dry and lifeless.

In late September, a killing frost came to the canyon. It bronzed the willows and touched the aspen with the first hints of gold. Vine maple on the hillsides turned brilliant russet. Then came the most glorious time of all in the mountains. Indian summer. Those few weeks sandwiched between the first frost and the actual beginnings of the cold weather. The air was crisp and tart as an apple. The southern skyline lay etched on the horizon—smoky, purple mountains against the pale blue sky. Each day was warm, at least in the sun, yet with a slight nip in the shaded corners of the canyon. And in the clear, cold nights the temperature dropped below freezing, glazing the grass with frozen dew which sparkled like diamonds in the full, yellow moonlight.

In October, Felis discovered the boy's trail again, leading from the cabin, down the canyon and across the hills to the village. School had started. She began to follow him once or twice a week and the cubs trailed along behind her. As usual, she turned off before reaching the village and went to the boulder overlooking the valley and the ranch.

But the old, peaceful days were gone. Felis had been seen by the rancher, who climbed the hill behind his ranch and discovered the pug marks—footprints—in the soft earth. The prints of an adult who had one toe missing, and the prints of four cubs. The rancher multiplied the bounty for each cougar—twenty-five dollars—by five. One hundred and twenty-five dollars. At first, he planned to set a trap on the rock, then discarded the idea. That would catch only one cougar and he wanted all of them. He thought and thought. What he needed was an alarm system which would alert him when the cougars appeared. So, in the end, he tied one of his hounds near the rock each day, with the expectation that if and when the cougars showed up, the hound would begin baying and the hunter could then run up the hill with the other dogs, tree all five of the cats, then shoot them, one by one.

A cougar's usual response to dogs is to climb a tree, to escape the dogs. Once treed, the cat is an easy target for the hunter.

But once in a while a cougar comes along who does not react in the usual way. Felis was one of them.

One morning late in October she led her little family into the area above the ranch. Unknown to her, one of the rancher's dogs was tied in the bushes near the rock. The hound happened to be asleep when the cougar family arrived. Felis went to her boulder and the cubs trotted into the bushes where they usually flopped to sleep while their mother lay on the rock. It was the same clump of bushes containing the dog. The male was the first one to enter the growth, so it was he who found the dog. In fact, he stepped on it. The hound came awake with a shrill yip. The male leaped back from the bushes with the dog after him. The cub stumbled and the hound had him. The other cubs scattered.

Felis whirled around from her place on the boulder, saw the situation and, in one bound, was in the bushes. She dragged the dog from her cub. The dog yowled with pain. Felis clawed him once, from tail to chin, and the dog fell dead in the bushes.

Then she took off, calling the cubs to her, racing over the mountain, through streams, along marshes, cutting across the territory of the male cougar who lived near the lake. Finally, she and the cubs arrived home late in the night. Exhausted, they flopped onto the rock overlooking the clearing and fell asleep.

Behind them, they left a trail which wound from the hill above the ranch and became lost in the tangle of trees in the male cougar's territory. The bounty hunter and his hounds found the trail after the dead dog was discovered.

Felis kept the family close to Burned Clearing for a week. Then hunger forced them to move out. The deer herd was grazing across the mountain in the no-man's land which lay between Felis' territory and that of the male cougar. One morning, she led the cubs through the saddle in the mountains which separated her from the deer.

The hunting was very good. After three tries, Felis brought down an old buck. When the family had eaten, she covered the carcass with dirt and branches and led the cubs back onto the ridge. There they found an overhang among the rocks where they slept. Late the following afternoon they came down to feed again. The two small female cubs trotted on ahead, anxious to be first at the carcass since they couldn't compete on equal terms with their larger sister and the male. At the edge of the clearing Felis stopped. Something had changed since she covered the deer the day before. She sniffed the air. There was an odor she remembered from many, many months earlier. From that day in the meadow when she had almost been killed. The odor. Man! And not only man, but the same man as on that terrifying day. And dogs! DANGER!

She wheeled and ran up the hill, calling the cubs to her. The male and the large female obeyed. The two small females ran out onto the clearing and began tearing at the deer meat.

Then the hounds came. From the far end of the meadow, they came running, baying in clear, loud voices. Straight for the two little cougar cubs. And behind them, the bounty hunter, a small man with a broken nose and tiny, pig-like eyes. Carrying a rifle and running behind his dogs.

The cougar cubs finally looked up, saw the hounds bearing down on them, and turned to run. They looked for their mother, but couldn't see her, didn't know that she was high on the hill, running with their sister and brother. The two little females dashed toward the trees, tried to run away, but the dogs were gaining rapidly. So they did what nature had equipped them to do. They climbed into a tree. The hounds ran up to the tree, barking, leaping up at the two cubs who sat looking down, their ears laid back, their eyes large with fear.

Felis and the remaining two cubs ran all the way to the ridge and the hidden overhang before they heard the rifle. *BANG! BANG!*

They spent the rest of the afternoon hiding and listening to the sounds which drifted up from the meadow—the hounds objecting as their owner leashed them, the man's curses as he tried to tie two little cougar bodies to the back of a frightened horse, and finally the jingle of a bridle and clip-clop of hoofs as the party left. When twilight came, the hillside was silent.

Felis led her two cubs back through the saddle and down to Burned Clearing.

They stayed with her for the following eighteen months. The spots of babyhood faded and the cubs developed the sleek, powerful bodies of hunters. Felis taught them to sneak in close to the deer, to lie in ambush, how to charge and drag down the prey. In winter they drifted with the deer to the lower range, and in spring, moved back to Burned Clearing. Then, when they were two years old, Felis drove them away. Their childhood was finished and the time had come for them to establish territories and families of their own. Felis wandered alone for a few months, then in early winter mated with the male who had sired the original litter of cubs.

She lived for sixteen years, longer than the average life span of cougars. In that time, she gave birth to seven litters, a total of twenty-five cubs born, almost all of whom died long before they reached adulthood. Only the strongest, the very best, survived. Accidents killed some, starvation and disease took others, and bounty hunting continued to exact its heavy toll.

In her lifetime, Felis was an important part of the canyon, helping to keep the deer and porcupine populations in balance with the available food supply. And when she died, she made a final contribution, returning her body's minerals and chemicals to the earth. The plants took these up for their own growth.

Season followed season, year in, year out. Winter's snow melted. The spring flowers appeared, thrived for a month or two, ripened, cast their seeds, then died back. Each year a new generation of babies was born to replace those which had gone before. Autumn came with its warm days and freezing nights. And winter returned. Life flowed on like a great river that has no beginning and no end. On and on.

PART III

Man and Cougar

For all but the last eight or nine thousand years of man's two million years on earth, he has been a hunter, following the game herds and living as any other predator. When the herds flourished, so did man; when catastrophe struck them, man also suffered.

During this time, man saw himself as a part of nature and a brother of the other creatures of the earth. He was willing to live and let live, sharing the herds with the other predators. In North America, they were wolves, cougar and bears, mainly. Because these two were so much a part of man's life, many myths sprang up about them.

To the Indians of Baja California, the cougar was

The cougar—hunter of deer, ghost cat, victim
of man's shortsighted misunderstanding.

one of the most revered of all animals, since it was he who supplied the people with meat, according to the legends. After a cougar had made a kill and covered it with brush, the buzzards would circle overhead, waiting to come down to feed. The Indians, seeing the buzzards, would follow them to the kill and eat the meat. Naturally, the people never killed or harmed cougars.

The Aztecs believed that death could be warded off by scratching one's breast with a bone from an albino cougar. Another myth claimed that urine from any of the great cats—cougars included—hardens into a precious stone called *lincurius*, and that the reason the cougar covers its urine is to keep man from finding this gem.

Among the Apaches, the wailing of a cougar was associated with death. Other Indians dangled a dried cougar's paw over a sick person's head to drive out the evil spirits which were causing the illness. Cougar gall was consumed by ill people to achieve the fierceness and strength of the cat and in order to drive away the illness. The Cochite Indians of New Mexico carved the cougar's likeness into rocks as images in a shrine.

About ten thousand years ago, man domesticated one of his fellow predators—the wolf. Wolves probably had been coming to early man's garbage dumps for many years to eat whatever leftover meat they could find. About 8000 B.C., they became part of the family—the first dogs. They discovered that they could eat just as well if man, not they, did the hunting. They gave up their freedom for security.

Not so the cats, who didn't join man for another six thousand years, and then only on their own terms. It happened in Egypt in approximately 1300 B.C. when small, wild cats were captured and domesticated.

Domestication for dogs and cats was quite different. First, since the dogs—or wolves—had lived in packs where there was one leader and many followers, those who came to join man could easily accept a strict social organization in which they were the bottom dog. Cats, on the other hand, came from a different background. With the exception of the African lion, cats are loners, each living apart from the other, subservient to no one. So the cats' relationship with their new companions was altogether different from the dogs' situation. Even to this day, cats appear to stay with man because they want to, not because they have to as is the case with dogs.

If a dog is abandoned by its master or lost from him, the odds are good that the dog will starve if he isn't picked up by someone. He simply can't take care of himself alone. But a cat does quite nicely when thrown on her own resources. In effect, we have bred the hunt out of dogs. Cats can revert to their wild ways on a moment's notice.

Perhaps it is this independent attitude which infuriates man about cats, even his own house cats. They simply will not come up to the master's side, lick his hand and beg for a bit of food. This seems to be quite bothersome to man's ego, since he likes to see himself as master of the earth and everything that lives on it.

Certain societies have deified cats. In ancient Egypt they were considered to be Bast, the goddess of the hunt, pleasure and love. Thousands of mummified cats have been found in tombs, along with mummified mice, presumably put there for the spirits of the cats to eat.

But if they have been revered in some societies, cats have been among the most cruelly mistreated of all animals in others, especially in Medieval Europe. There, they were thought to be allied with Satan and were subjected to the most inhumane abuses. And if they happened to be black, they were even worse treated and were assumed to be one with witches. During those superstitious times, people actually organized hunts to run down and kill cats. And all of this happened during a period when cats probably were among man's best friends. Great plagues and epidemics were sweeping across Europe, often carried by rats and other rodents. Cats killed them by the hundreds of thousands, perhaps keeping the epidemics from being worse than they were. But to the superstitious minds of the people, the cats still were symbols of evil and must be destroyed.

Before laughing at these silly ideas, we should remember that remnants of these superstitions still linger, even today. Many people believe that if a person's path is crossed by a black cat, that person will have bad luck of some kind. And the black cat as the symbol of the witch's companion on Halloween is a legend that comes to us directly from the Middle Ages.

Perhaps the hatred which the white man had for cougars from the moment he first contacted them in the western hemisphere came in part from those old legends and superstitions he lived with in Europe. And those, in turn, maybe came from still earlier times.

Early in his development of civilization, man's attitude about wild animals, especially the predators, underwent a dramatic change. During the long ages when he was a hunter, he accepted them as fellow-creatures who lived on the game animals, just as he did. But about nine thousand years ago man discovered that he could establish a more reliable source of food by herding animals than by hunting them. Man the hunter became man the pastoralist.

Now, it was one thing for man the hunter to share the wild animals with the other predators. It was quite another thing for him to share his own domestic herds. So the other predators suddenly became enemies, thieves who tried to steal what belonged to man. His response was to kill them. And the killing is still going on.

It caused the African lion to disappear from all of southern Europe and the Near East by the time of Christ. Wolves were gone from England by the beginning of the sixteenth century and from Scotland by the eighteenth. By 1940 they were extinct in the eastern part of the United States except for two small populations in Wisconsin and Michigan. Until 1970, the government of the Soviet Union had as its official policy the elimination of all wolves in Russia. Fortunately, they now see the animals as a national heritage and have placed them on the protected list.

Cougars have fared no better than the other predators. As mentioned earlier, at one time they had the largest range of any mammal in the western hemisphere, from the Atlantic to the Pacific, and from southern Canada all the way to the very tip of South America. They lived in jungles and deserts and from sea level to the highest mountains. That was before the white man declared his war on them.

Admittedly, they must have been a terrifying surprise to the early white settlers of America. Their unearthly screams could be heard deep in the forest. They killed cattle, horses and sheep. Yet they were only rarely seen. So stories began to be woven about the mysterious ghost cats who inhabited the wilderness. It was said that they deliberately imitated the screams of women and babies in order to lure would-be rescuers into the forests where they were torn to pieces by the cats. Cougars, the stories claimed, lay in wait along game trails, then leaped on innocent victims, always choosing pregnant females or babies, dragging them down in a bloodthirsty lust for killing.

On and on went the stories about the cougar, always filled with misinformation and sounding strangely similar to the older stories about wild animals in Europe where the settlers had come from. And when the people began the great western movement across the continent, they took the stories with them. Children were taught about the horrible creatures who lived in the wilderness and gradually, hatred and fear of cougars became part of the tradition of the people. Destroy them!

For four hundred years the killing went on while North America was being conquered and settled. When the continent was finally won, only small, remnant populations of the great cats were left. And that is where the situation stands today—perhaps eighteen thousand cougar left in North America, living in the most inaccessible parts of the continent. Their numbers are decreasing and unless they are protected by law, we will lose them.

At one time, a case could have been made for the elimination of individual cougars which attacked domestic livestock. But there never was a reasonable excuse for the wholesale slaughter of an entire species.

Man has devised several methods to kill cougars. One of the earliest was the pit hunt, in which a large hole was dug, covered with twigs and leaves, then baited with a live goat or sheep. When the cougar tried to reach the bait, it fell through the covering into the pit, the bottom of which often was armed with pointed sticks on which the cat was impaled. In South America, the bola was used to bring down, not only cougar but other animals of the pampas. The bola is a long rope which has three or more ends. On each of the ends is a heavy stone. The hunter swings his bola around his head then releases it much as a lariat is thrown. The end ropes wrap themselves around the prey's legs, trapping him. Cougars were run down from horseback and trapped with bolas.

The Indians used a technique of hunting predators which has become popular with today's "varmint callers." This is the method of calling the animal to the hunter by simulating the squeal of a rabbit in pain. The Indians used crude instruments to produce the sound. Modern varmint callers use sophisticated whistles and even electronic instruments. These "sportsmen" kill anything that shows up—coyotes, bobcats, lynxes, cougars. The predators move in thinking they will get a meal. Instead, they get a bullet between the eyes. This is considered great sport by some people.

Cougars also are trapped and poisoned, but the most common method of hunting them is with dogs. Usually, the cats climb a tree to escape the hounds, then the hunter shoots them. Very simple.

One of the latest lion hunting methods caters exclusively to the trophy hunters—those "sportsmen" who set out to kill animals merely to say they have killed them, and perhaps to display their heads or pelts on a "game room" wall. Since the war against cougars has been so very successful, the usual method of hunting a free, wild animal with dogs has become increasingly difficult and unproductive. So a few enterprising guides have set out to guarantee their clients a cougar. They have trapped the animals and kept them confined to cages. Then, when their client is ready, the cats are released and shot. Fortunately, these "canned" hunts appeal to only a small minority of the trophy hunters.

From the earliest colonial days the hunting of cougars was encouraged by the bounty system. The government paid money for each cougar killed. It is a poor system which is subject to great abuse. For instance, often the animal being bountied was not killed in the state or county where payment was claimed, but was brought in from another area where there was no bounty or a much smaller one.

Over the years, as the number of cougars has diminished, the states have repealed their bounties. In 1970, Arizona abolished its bounty on cougars. It was the last state to have such a bounty, so finally, the system is dead.

But all the hunting of whatever kind cannot account for the appalling decrease in the number of cougars. There is another cause, even more important. It is the steady destruction of the wilderness areas which the cougar needs as a home. Most of the forests in the eastern part of the United States are gone. The plains are plowed under and their bison destroyed. All that is left are the few islands of wilderness in the West, and that is where the last of the cougars still live, excepting the tiny population in Florida's Everglades.

During the past few years there has been a movement to save cougars. In Florida, the animal is fully protected and anyone killing one of them is arrested. In a few of the western states the cougar has been declared a game animal, subject to hunting restrictions imposed by fish and game departments. But in only one or two states have closed seasons been established, that is, times when the cat may not be hunted. So, without a closed season, the protection offered by game animal status means very little. There are indications that some of the states and even the federal government will finally protect the few cougars which are left.

But it is not only the hunting which has to be changed. There are attitudes which must be changed also. Even with the bounty removed, certain people still delight in killing the cats. They run them down with snowmobiles, following along behind the dogs, then shoot the cats when they are treed. Or they play the varmint caller game. They seem dedicated to erasing the last vestige of cougars, and in that regard they are like the late Ben Lilly, a government hunter who was paid by the federal government to seek out and kill cougars. Lilly was very successful. He killed more than one thousand cougars and claimed that he would have done so even if he hadn't been paid to do it. He saw himself as an instrument of God, ridding the world of vermin.

Of course, Lilly had a distorted, even a sick view of the situation, but there is something in it which is similar to the "normal" man's relationship with wild animals. He sees himself as better than they, as the finest possible expression of life. This smug attitude then allows him to see other forms of life as "vermin."

While man lived as a hunter, he held no such attitude. He knew that he was just one of countless expressions of life. Today, the situation is much different. Man lives removed from nature for the most part, and this has distorted his picture of himself. Most people breathe an atmosphere which bears little resemblance to fresh air. All of their food comes from supermarkets. They seldom walk any place, preferring to drive their cars. They live surrounded by concrete and iron. What have they to do with nature?

Yet, the truth is that each of us, man and cougar, eagle and ant, whale and phytoplankton is a part, and only a part of the natural processes of the universe. No one of us lives completely independent of every other bit of life. Man might see himself as removed from this intimate relationship, but he is as much a partner in life as any other living being. This is his heritage and he cannot escape it.

Consider his relationship with bacteria, one of the

smallest of all life forms. Man depends on bacteria, specifically, on the bacteria which live in his intestines and which break down his food so that he can use it. It doesn't matter at all whether he lives in the most modern city in the world or in a cave in the mountains. He is absolutely dependent on those bacteria.

He is also tied to the phytoplankton—the microscopic plants floating freely in the ocean. They produce seventy-five per cent of the world's oxygen, and man, like all animals, cannot live without oxygen to breathe.

Man needs to eat food. So do all other animals. He needs reasonably clean air to breathe and water to drink. So do other animals. He needs to survive into adulthood in order to reproduce and continue the species. So do the other animals.

The things which unite life are much more important than the things which seem to divide it.

What has this to do with cougars?

Just this: they, as we, are part of the natural processes, and they, as we, deserve to live out their role.

Man set out to exterminate cougars because he saw them as a threat to his livestock. And it is true that cougars kill sheep, cattle and horses. Not many, to be sure. But they do kill them.

Yet, as conservationist Commander Peter Scott said recently, "Man is the most dangerous predatory animal that ever stalked the earth." Because of man, *one species of plant or animal slips into oblivion each nine months!* And once a species is gone, it is gone forever.

So what? What difference would it make if every wild animal on earth disappeared?

Many people believe that we need the wild animals—those we once called brothers—just as we need air and water and food. We need them to learn more about ourselves, our illnesses and social habits.

We need them to learn more about ecology, that science which studies the relationships between everything that exists on earth. Since we are part of these relationships, we must learn all we can about them for our own welfare, if for no other reason. Who knows in what delicate ways the great mass of life is looped together? Who knows in what peril we place ourselves and the entire world by our endless muddling?

Finally, we need animals in a less obvious way.

Man, as a part of life, began his existence about two billion years ago in the form of protoplasm floating in the sea. With infinite patience and persistence, this fragile glob of life hung on and inched its way upward, becoming more complex, more able to control its movements. Countless evolutionary mistakes were cast aside and the few successes pushed on.

It took time, thousands of millions of years during which continents rose from the sea, settled back and rose again. Mountains thrust their peaks skyward, were worn back by the water and wind, and new mountains took their place. Massive sheets of ice inched from the polar regions, covered the land, then withdrew.

Through all of this enormous shifting of the land, life hung on, a brash intruder in the universe. It multiplied, changed to meet the changing conditions, fanned out to fit into every conceivable ecological niche. It crawled, hopped, flew, swam, jumped, burrowed, ran and eventually it walked upright on two feet. Man.

So far as we know, we appeared about two million years ago in Africa. We fought our way from the grasslands and spread out over the entire globe. We increased our numbers until today there are three billion of us. And our very numbers constitute the single greatest threat to the earth.

Now we live in cities, far removed from the basic

struggles for existence. We have been civilized for ten thousand years. It sounds like a long time. But, in terms of our two million years of life, it is merely an eyewink. Yet, because of the life we now lead, we assume that we are separate from nature. The memory of what we are and where we came from burns low at times. We need living reminders outside of ourselves to tell us that we are still a part of the great, living river of life. Wild animals living in the wilderness can help. It doesn't matter very much whether or not we ever get to see one of them. Just to know that they are there as part of our heritage is enough.

The fact that we created civilization is not, in itself, bad. Because of it, you and I live reasonably comfortable lives. What is bad is that we have forsaken that other part of ourselves—the natural part. We see ourselves as apart from, rather than a part of the natural processes of the earth.

Cougars and other wild animals can help us. All we have to do is let them live.

In Appreciation

In writing what I hope is an accurate, honest story about cougars, I have drawn heavily on the findings of a handful of naturalists and ethologists—the scientists who study animal behavior. These dedicated people have spent hundreds of hours in the wilderness, searching for cougars, trailing them and trying to assemble meaningful information from the clues they have found. It is only recently that we have conducted serious field studies on cougars. Without the information which comes from such work, we will be hard pressed to give the cats the protection they need if they are to survive.

So I want to thank some of the people whose work has contributed so much to an understanding of the cougar, and who made it possible for me to write the story of Felis. The first is Maurice G. Hornocker, who spent several winters in the wilderness of Idaho trapping and tagging a cougar population in order to study its territorial and predation habits. Then, there are people who conducted earlier studies—Stanley P. Young, W. Leslie Robinette and Edward J. Connolly, Jr. A special "Thank you" goes to my friend, Ferris Weddle, the naturalist/writer who graciously opened his home and his files of cougar information to me. Finally, thanks to John Harris and Don Beattie, of the North American Association for the Preservation of Predatory Animals, and their friend, Sombra the cougar, who was the model for Felis.

INDEX

African lions, 12, 20, 22, 139

babies, *see* infants
baboons, 25
badgers, 53-55
bears, winter behavior of, 79
beavers, 57-58, 126-127
    winter behavior of, 78
behavior patterns, 25.
    See also reproduction;
    territoriality; winter, effect of
birds
    juncos, 70
    lapwings' territoriality,
      40-41
    migrations, 70-71, 78
    ptarmigans, 79
    red-tailed hawks' eyesight,
      37-38
    reproduction, 92
    songs, 42
bounty system, *see* hunting
    for cougars

carnivores, 20, 24. *See also*
    specific animals
catamounts, 24
cats
    abuse of, 137-138
    compared with dogs, 21-22,
      137
    deification of, 137
    domesticated, 136-137
    hunting style, 22
    social life, 22
    see also specific animals
cheetahs, 14
civets, 21
cold-blooded animals, hiber-
    nation of, 78.
    See also specific animals
color blindness, 115
coloration, protective, 79-80
Columbus, Christopher, 11
cougars
    life span, 133
    names for, 24
    physical appearance, 14-18,
      23, 39
    population, current, 18

scientific classification, 24
social life, 22
see also specific subjects
cubs, *see* infants

death rates, 66-67
deer, 69, 80
deer tigers, 24
Dinictis, 18-20
dogs
    compared with cats, 21-22,
      137
    domesticated, 136, 137
    evolution of, 21
    hunting style, 22
    social life, 22
domestication of animals,
    136-137
dreams, animals', 33

elephants, gestation period
    of, 87
elks, rutting season, 69
ethology, *see* behavior
evolution
    of cougars, 18-21
    during Ice Ages, 77
extinction of animals, 77, 139.
    See also death rates; hunting
    for cougars
eyes
    of cougars, 23
    of *Felis* group, 21
    of *Leo* group, 20
    see also eyesight
eyesight
    color blindness, 115
    of cougar cubs, 99
    of red-tailed hawks, 37-38
    see also eyes

family life, cougars', 35-37
Felis concolor, 24
Felis group, 20-21
fights, *see* "wars,"
    territorial
first order consumers, 65
fish, *see* sticklebacks
food, cougars', *see* hunting,
    cougars'

About the Author

Robert Gray, an active conservationist and nature lover, spent much of his boyhood outdoors. After a six-year stint in the Navy, in which he saw action in the Pacific during World War II, he spent two years in Alaska as a free-lance writer and photographer.

Born in Butte, Montana, Mr. Gray holds a B.A. degree in Fine Arts, English and Education from the San Diego State College. He has done graduate work in Fine Arts at the University of Southern California.

His varied career includes two years as the Assistant Public Relations Director for the San Diego Zoo, and two years as a farmer and free-lance writer on a forty-acre farm in Oregon. He is currently the Community Services Director of the San Diego Mesa College. Formerly he was Executive Director of the Elsa Wild Animal Appeal of the United States, an organization founded by Joy Adamson to enlist children in conservation.

Mr. and Mrs. Gray and their young son make their home in San Diego, California.

What the critics say about Robert Gray's books

CHILDREN OF THE ARK
The Rescue of the World's Vanishing Wildlife

". . . informative and interesting . . ."
The ALA Booklist

THE GREAT APES
The Natural Life of Chimpanzees, Gorillas, Orangu-
tans, and Gibbons

". . . an in-depth treatment of the most current ecological and ethological findings concerning each of
the great apes and problems associated with their
conservation . . . the book is well written . . ."

Library Journal

GRAY WOLF
The Natural Life of North American Wolves

"The natural history of the North American Gray
Wolf, presented in a lively, entertaining manner."

Library Journal